FINANCING SMALL ENTERPRISE

*Proceedings of a seminar organized
by the Netherlands Development
Finance Company (FMO)*

Edited by Malcolm Harper and M.F. de Jong

**Practical
ACTION
PUBLISHING**

INTERMEDIATE TECHNOLOGY PUBLICATIONS 1986

Practical Action Publishing Ltd
25 Albert Street, Rugby, CV21 2SD, Warwickshire, UK
www.practicalactionpublishing.com

© Intermediate Technology Publications 1986

First published 1986\Digitised 2013

ISBN 10: 0 946688 82 6
ISBN 13 Paperback: 9780946688821
ISBN Library Ebook: 9781780442204
Book DOI: https://doi.org/10.3362/9781780442204

A catalogue record for this book is available from the British Library.

Since 1974, Practical Action Publishing has published and disseminated books
and information in support of international development work throughout
the world. Practical Action Publishing is a trading name of Practical Action
Publishing Ltd (Company Reg. No. 01159018), the wholly owned publishing
company of Practical Action. Practical Action Publishing trades only in support
of its parent charity objectives and any profits are covenanted back to Practical
Action (Charity Reg. No. 247257, Group VAT Registration No. 880 9924 76).

Reasonable efforts have been made to publish reliable data and information,
but the author and publisher cannot assume responsibility for the validity of all
materials or for the consequences of their use.

The manufacturer's authorised representative in the EU for product safety is
Lightning Source France, 1 Av. Johannes Gutenberg, 78310 Maurepas, France.
compliance@lightningsource.fr

CONTENTS

PREFACE

In September 1985 the Netherlands Development Finance Company
(FMO) organized a two-day seminar on the theme: the viability
of small-scale enterprise development financing institutions.

Thirty-five representatives from developing countries and
from national and international donor agencies met in The Hague
to discuss the prospects and problems related to the provision
of credit to small-scale entrepreneurs in developing countries.
Participants' reactions confirmed that the meeting would be an
effective platform for practitioners to present and exchange
their views and opinions. While the seminar did not produce a
major breakthrough, we neverthelesss believe that the
proceedings were of sufficient interest to warrant distribution
beyond the participating institutions. FMO therefore invited
the Chairman, Professor Malcolm Harper, and Mr. Martin F. de
Jong, head of FMO's small-scale enterprise development
department, to edit the papers and the proceedings, and to
present them in the form of this book.

We are grateful to the seminar participants who spoke so
frankly and clearly, and to the speakers, whose presentations
are reproduced in this book.

Prof. Malcolm Harper
Martin F. de Jong

INTRODUCTION

FMO and Small-Scale Enterprise

The Netherlands Development Finance Company (FMO) is a development finance company and is not normally concerned with organizing seminars. In fact, this seminar on the viability of Small-Scale Enterprise Development Finance Institutions (SSE-DFIs) was the first meeting of its kind to be organized by FMO.

The main objective of FMO is to 'make a contribution to the advancement of productive enterprises in developing countries'. In 1978 the company decided that the promotion of local entrepreneurship fell within the scope of this definition.

It was determined from the beginning that FMO's normal lending criteria would have to apply to the development of small enterprise, and that the provision of credit would have to be the main activity involved.

Since FMO does not normally make loans for less than Dfl. 500,000 (approximately US$ 200,000), it became necessary to identify a local intermediary organization in the relevant Third World country through which FMO's assistance could be delivered. This institution would have to have the character of a financing institution, without excluding the possibility of providing other services as well.

In view of FMO's existing relationships with a number of local development banks, it appeared logical to seek their collaboration in the promotion of small enterprises. These development banks, however, because of their policies, their resources and their organizational structures, were often not suitable intermediaries for the promotion of small enterprises. For other reasons, commercial banks, post office savings banks, savings and credit associations or local moneylenders were no more feasible.

Other solutions, therefore, had to be found. In the seven years in which FMO has been working in this field, two alternatives have been developed:
- a completely new institution has been created, in cooperation with the local development bank and other local and international sources of finance
- an independent small enterprise promotion department has been set up within a development bank.

We have used the term small-scale enterprise development finance institutions, or SSE-DFI, to describe both types of intermediary.

To date, FMO has participated in financing nine SSE-DFIs. It expects annually to add two more such institutions over the next few years.

FMO has committed well over Dfl. 35 million to these SSE-DFIs, and it expects to increase this by at least Dfl. 10 million a year. The total finance available to the nine institutions is well over Dfl. 100 million, since FMO on average contributes between 20 and 30 per cent of the total resources. The total number of enterprises financed by the SSE-DFIs will reach 1,000 in 1985, and is rapidly increasing.

Some broad guidelines have evolved as a result of FMO's experiences in relation to small enterprises. For example, it is essential that a strong local institution, in general a development bank, should participate. The operations should start on a limited basis, to allow for the gradual growth of the institution and its staff, and during this process policies can develop, procedures can be introduced and knowledge about the market for small enterprise financing can be acquired. A high priority should be placed on the development of local management and local decision-making capability.

No two SSE-DFIs, however, are identical. So far as is known to FMO, none of them have confined themselves only to financial or banking services. They offer a wide range of other services, including management accounting and production advice to entrepreneurs, and the leasing of premises and equipment. Some SSE-DFIs provide these forms of non-financial assistance themselves, while others have set up subsidiaries for the purpose.

The SSE-DFIs also adopt a wide variety of practices in relation to the way in which small enterprises are charged for financial and non-financial services. Nearly all the institutions depend heavily on foreign funds, and the effect of this on their long-term viability is still unknown. It seems obvious that local finances should form an increasing part of the required funding, but it is difficult to see how these local resources can become available if the institutions charge interest rates which are insufficient to cover the cost of funds, the high risks and the high operating costs involved. In these circumstances, it is necessary to ask whether the non-governmental character of the institutions can or should be maintained.

The focus of the seminar, therefore, was on the question of whether newly established small enterprise development finance institutions can survive in the long run, and, if so, under what conditions. This theme can be summarized as 'the viability of SSE-DFIs'.

Scope and limitations of the seminar

Thirty-five people participated in the seminar: 14 represented institutions in developing countries which specialize in financing and assisting small enterprises, and which have an association with FMO, while 15 represented lending or other donor organizations which work or intend to work with small enterprises, and which are associated with at least one of the institutions receiving assistance from the FMO. There were in addition six representatives of bilateral organizations from The Netherlands and elsewhere, which have a particular interest in this field.

2

As a result, the participants, with few exceptions, have some link with FMO in the field of small enterprise promotion. A number of them however, have far wider experience in the field, far beyond the projects in which they are associated with FMO. As a result of their presence, it became clear that FMO's definition of an SSE-DFI was too narrow. The discussion, therefore, did not focus on SSE-DFIs as if they were the only intermediary for providing finance to small enterprises, but on all types of institutions which could be created or used for this purpose. The scope of the seminar was therefore widened, and the theme could perhaps have been more aptly described as 'financing small enterprises, institutional constraints and opportunities'.

A number of issues, although their importance was recognized, were nevertheless completely omitted from the discussions or only briefly mentioned, since they could have distracted attention from the main theme. The most important of these were: the role of government in small enterprise development, the need for coordination, the need for non-financial assistance, and the informal sector, or micro-enterprises.

Governments have a most important role to play. They determine the business climate as their policies and regulations act either in favour or, as often seems to be the case, against the development of entrepreneurship. Some of the experiences which are related indicate that governments actually constrain the development of small enterprises. This can be done by excessive regulations, which lead entrepreneurs to prefer to remain in the informal sector, and thus to disqualify themselves from receiving assistance from small enterprise development programmes. In addition governments often create or work through large, centralized, inflexible and top-down institutions or departments which cannot reach small enterprises effectively.

The participants recognized that government policies are important, but that only a minority of the largest donors are in a position to discuss issues of this kind with governments of recipient countries when they are negotiating large financial packages. SSE-DFIs and donors nevertheless may have a responsibility to remind governments of how they can contribute by establishing a better policy environment, and thus to encourage them to create a climate which is more conducive to the development of small enterprise.

It seems obvious that there should be coordination between the agencies and institutions involved in small enterprise development at the local and international level but, as the Chairman put it, 'this may be a chimaera'. There is very little that one institution can do about the activities of another. Institutions should therefore concentrate on what they themselves are doing and accept the existing environment. If nobody else is providing a service which is deemed to be indispensable, the SSE-DFI may well consider providing this

3

service itself, as a number of the SSE-DFIs in fact do. In addition, competition between small enterprise assistance programmes is not necessarily a bad thing, unless it is merely a matter of competition between the levels of subsidy offered.

The key to small enterprise development is the entrepreneur. The role of donors and SSE-DFIs is at best peripheral and modest and the majority of enterprises are never reached by them. Although entrepreneurs often claim that lack of credit is their most important problem, finance may not be the most important service. Non-financial services should therefore not be overlooked. If government or other agencies set up for the purpose do not offer them, SSE-DFIs may have to provide these services in addition to credit, which is their main task.

Experience in a number of countries suggests that in the long run governments will have to play a role in the provision of non-financial services to small enterprises, possibly through subsidies. This does not mean that technical assistance, training, extension and advice to small enterprises are not or should not be provided for a fee, when this is possible.

There is a possibility, when an SSE-DFI both participates in a client's equity and provides advisory services, of tax benefits for the client to pay for the technical assistance out of pre-tax earnings, rather than dividends after tax.

It is necessary to investigate further whether non-financial services make it easier to provide credit. If so, the provision of such services could be a powerful argument to encourage commercial bankers to lend money to small businesses.

The seminar was concerned with the viability of SSE-DFIs in developing countries. We therefore considered the target client group to include only enterprises which qualify for investment credit from financial institutions and which are part of the formal sector. Small enterprises in the informal sector, or micro-enterprises, are therefore in most cases effectively excluded, although some of the institutions represented at the seminar do in some cases provide very small loans to this form of business.

This should not be taken to mean that it is impossible to finance micro-enterprises on a viable basis. There are a number of very successful micro-enterprise lending schemes and, indeed, a number of dismal failures in the financing of formal small businesses. There is no evidence to suggest that the larger the enterprises financed, the more viable will be the financing institution. Nevertheless, SSE-DFIs, which in many respects resemble the development banks which created them, are unlikely to be able to play a significant role in financing micro-enterprises.

In so far as the above issues were discussed at the seminar, the conclusions might be summarized as follows:
- the role of government should be taken for granted
- energy spent on trying to attain coordination would be better

spent on the actual promotion of small enterprises
- it is often necessary for SSE-DFIs to provide non-financial
  services, and this influences their viability
- the vast majority of very small entrepreneurs are not reached
  by the institutions which were represented at the seminar.

The programme

The seminar focused on the question of whether or not it is
possible for an SSE-DFI to be viable in the long run, without
subsidies. The answer to this question will eventually depend
on the profit and loss statement of the institution concerned.
The main theme was therefore divided into three sub-themes,
each reflecting a part of the profit and loss statement:

1. Interest rate policies
2. The optimum mix of financial resources
3. Transaction costs

The viability of any lending institution depends to a large
extent on the interest rates which are charged. How should
interest rates reflect the shortage of capital and the risk and
effort involved in small enterprise financing, and how far, if
at all, should small enterprises be subsidized through low
interest loans?

An SSE-DFI has to choose an optimum mix of financial
resources, by seeking the right balance between foreign and
domestic funds, loans and deposits and equity and loans. These
decisions are influenced by the availability and costs of the
long-term finance, and the short-term solutions may be
different from those which are preferred in the long-term.

It is necessary to accept that it is expensive to finance
small enterprises; the transaction costs involved in a small
loan may well be the same as those for a loan of ten or more
times the amount, other services may have to be provided before
and during the lifetime of the loan, and the bad debt level may
exceed double figures.

Each of the speakers presented a paper and after each
presentation participants had an opportunity to ask for
clarifications. In addition each theme was concluded by
general discussions. Contributions from developing countries
and donor agencies were balanced in order to encourage an
exchange of views and experiences; this exchange continued
during breaks between the sessions and after the seminar
itself. These informal discussions obviously do not form part
of these proceedings, although we hope that they may have been
very fruitful, for SSE-DFIs and for donors alike.

Chapter 1 of this book reproduces the presentations by
individual speakers, and in chapter 2 the discussions which
followed the presentations are summarized, together with the
Chairman's concluding remarks. A summary statement of the
operations of the SSE-DFIs which were involved is given in the

appendix. The seminar programme and a full list of the names
and addresses of the participants is included at the end of the
book as a stimulus for a continued exchange of ideas and
information.

1. THE PRESENTATIONS

KEYNOTE SPEECH: THE ROLE OF THE INSTITUTION

M.F. DE JONG
Head SSE Department
Netherlands Development Finance Company (FMO)
The Netherlands

INTRODUCTION

Concern with finance for small enterprise may appear to be a rather recent phenomenon, but in many ways it is not. It is possible to put the issue in a historical perspective and to compare what is happening in developing countries with The Netherlands, although not in every way. We can contrast, for instance, the success of the Marshall plan in rebuilding industrial Europe after the Second World War, with the industrial policies which have been adopted by so many developing countries in the hope that something similar would happen there as well.

It appears that, in part at any rate, these policies were not successful because of a lack of a tradition of entrepreneurship in developing countries. In addition to the more commonly used justifications for stimulating the development of small enterprises, such as the creation and distribution of income and jobs, the utilization of local resources and avoidance of capital intensity, the promotion of entrepreneurship and local management skills is a critical element in the development process. In the task of stimulating the development of small enterprises the quality of the responsible agencies is possibly the most important factor in determining failure or success.

There are a number of reasons why longer established financial institutions are not always in the best position to assist in the development of small enterprises. For that reason, it is sometimes necessary to create new specialist organizations; for convenience, these are grouped under the general term of Small-Scale Enterprise Development Finance Institutions, or SSE-DFIs.

Because subsidized seed capital and finance may be needed to start and run an SSE-DFI donor funds may be essential. Not all types of such funds are equally appropriate for building a strong SSE-DFI. Everyone working on the development of small enterprises, on a donor or developing country side, should treat the development of effective institutions of this type as a matter of highest priority. In the long run, small enterprises and donors will be best served by viable and effective financing institutions.

A HISTORIAL PERSPECTIVE

Industrial development policies in most developing countries during the 20 years following the Second World War paid little attention to local entrepreneurs. Industrial development meant the development of large-scale industry; government policies resulted in the development of a small number of capital intensive and import-dependent industries. In many countries such policies are still effectively in force.

The main financial institutions were for some years commercial banks of which many were foreign owned, specializing mainly in the financing of import and export trade. The financial sector was gradually expanded by the establishment of national development finance companies. Multilateral and bilateral donors played an important role in the establishment of these finance companies and their major role was to provide the long-term foreign exchange which was needed for investment in the new large-scale industries. The majority of their clients were these larger companies which were initially intended to substitute for imports and have more recently been targeted towards export markets.

It was perhaps to be expected that the need to stimulate local entrepreneurship should first have been recognized in Gandhi's India. The issue of small enterprise, as far as we know, was first discussed at an international level during the Asian Regional Conference in 1957 in New Delhi. In 1961 the International Labour Office first demonstrated its interest in this field by publishing <u>Services for Small Scale Industries</u>, and the UN Industrial Development Organization followed in 1969 with the monograph entitled <u>Small Scale Industry</u>.

The World Bank, which had been instrumental in the establishment of most of the development finance companies, was the first financial donor agency to take a special interest in the development of small enterprise. Two small loans related to this field were made to Pakistan, and in 1973 the World Bank made a US$ 30 million loan to a development finance company in India, for on-lending to small enterprises. In 1975 the World Bank officially recognized small enterprises as a major element in industrial development. It is thus true to say that the issue of finance for small enterprise in developing countries has only recently gained recognition, at least among international donors.

In industrialized countries, however, institutional finance for small enterprise has a far longer history. In the Netherlands a number of small private banks were started in various regional centres in the nineteenth century and they provided, among other services, credit to small businesses. These banks appear to have been effective and profitable because they knew their clients well and ownership of the banks themselves passed from father to son. The banks' main criterion for lending money was their intimate knowledge of the entrepreneur; the appraisal and monitoring procedures used today were virtually unknown.

In 1927 the government of the Netherlands was instrumental in amalgamating 25 of these smaller banks to form the Netherlands Bank for Small and Medium Business (NMB). The government has remained the major shareholder, but is at present considering disposing of its 16 per cent shareholding in the NMB. This demonstrates that small enterprise financing requires special treatment everywhere.

The promotion of small enterprises in developing countries is thus of concern to governments, industry associations, trade unions, banks and donors. Governments have too often paid only lip-service to the stimulation of local business and have relied on cheap credit alone to perform the task. Chambers of Commerce, Employers Federations and other associations have too often failed to include small enterprises in their membership. Trade Unions have rarely been represented amongst the employees of small enterprises and banks have often been ill-equipped, or not interested, to make very small, high risk and unsecured loans. Donors also have their problems and are searching for ways and means to assist in the process of stimulating small enterprise.

There are, however, many difficulties; small enterprises are not a homogenous group and, unlike farmers, it is difficult to generalize about them. The very definition of what is and what is not a small enterprise is far from clear; a study undertaken in 1975 suggested that there were 75 different definitions, from 50 different countries.

CREDIT FOR SMALL ENTERPRISES - THE INSTITUTION

Credit is an essential element in the development of small enterprises and entrepreneurs themselves blame many of their problems on their limited access to credit. Why is credit not more accessible to small businesses?

There are enormous differences, in every respect, between well-established institutions such as banks and local small-scale entrepreneurs. In many cases they probably would not even agree as to what the enterprise itself actually entails. For the entrepreneur this may well include his household property, his farm and his family. He may have to resist pressure from his peers in his effort to improve, he keeps no records and his enterprise is an extension of himself which includes everything he owns and all his social and family obligations. The bank, however, will tend to reflect its history and its original owners. It is a western oriented and business-like organization. The gaps in understanding and operation are obvious.

It is clear that there are enormous differences between financing joint ventures, foreign or state owned companies and large-scale industries, and credit for small enterprises. It is necessary to introduce new instruments to bridge the gap and no completely satisfactory answer has yet been found.

In pursuance of its development objectives FMO has participated in the establishment and development of nine SSE-DFIs since 1978, and it is expected that two more will be added each year for the next ten years. To date, these initiatives have either involved the creation of a completely new institution, in cooperation with the local development bank and other local and international sources of finance, or the setting up of an independently operating department within an existing development bank.

FMO's experience so far suggests that the commercial banks and the development finance companies were right to be cautious in this field. It is expensive and risky to make credit available to small enterprises, and credit has to be accompanied by extension services and training, and the whole operation cannot be commerically viable if it must depend on a spread of no more than one or two per cent between the cost of the sources and the interest to be charged. It appears, therefore, that the interest rates charged by private moneylenders probably reflect the prevailing commercial realities of small enterprise finance.

There is one critical difference between the SSE-DFIs such as those with which the FMO has been involved and the NMB, the Netherlands bank which was referred to earlier. The NMB was originally initiated from the 'bottom up' by a number of private banking entrepreneurs; the SSE-DFIs have been started by donors and development finance companies, from the 'top down'. As a result, the SSE-DFIs, whether they are independent organizations or departments, resemble development finance companies in their organization, their staffing, their salary structures, their methods of supervision and evaluation and their ownership.

If an SSE-DFI is to be an effective link between its founding bankers and its client enterprises, it will have to identify itself at least in part with local entrepreneurs, who are the traditional sources of finance for local enterprise. It may in fact be advisable for local entrepreneurs to take a financial stake in an SSE-DFI; this may not necessarily lead to better repayment but it may develop local roots for the SSE-DFI and reduce dependence on foreign donors. It may also be advisable for the DFI to establish working relationships with local moneylenders since they are an obvious means of bridging the gap. Whatever approaches are adopted, it is clear that there is no single solution, and that no perfect answer has yet been found.

THE ROLE OF FINANCIERS

What then is the role of the founders and financiers of an SSE-DFI? Local development finance companies may be politically required to be involved. If such a company participates, it clearly takes upon itself the role of the most important parent of the SSE-DFI, and failure may well have a negative impact on

10

the parent. Local development finance corporations thus have a vital interest in the viability and continuity of SSE-DFIs in which they are involved.

The role of foreign donors is less clear. Their contribution, indeed, may make it less possible to create a viable SSE-DFI. Firstly, donor contributions are often in the form of grants rather than loans; the SSE-DFIs repayment capacity is therefore irrelevant and the pressure for viability is reduced. Even if the donor contribution is lent rather than given, it often has to be channelled through, or at least guaranteed by, the government which becomes the debtor rather than the SSE-DFI. In several cases this seriously constrains the SSE-DFI in its policies, particularly in relation to interest rates, so that subsidized credit is the result. Donors also impose strong pressures for rapid disbursement in order to achieve technical results in terms of actual small businesses. This pressure may seriously inhibit the development of a viable long-term institution.

It is clear, therefore, that there is some risk that not all the founders and financiers of an SSE-DFI may be equally committed to building a strong institution. Donor agencies in particular may prefer to bypass the SSE-DFI, either because it involves extra cost or because the establishment of the institution leads to a considerable delay in the disbursement of funds. There may even be a direct conflict between establishing a viable SSE-DFI and implementing actual small enterprise 'projects'.

VIABILITY

'Viability' is subjective. Fundamentally, an SSE-DFI is viable if its financiers agree that it is. This is clearly unsatisfactory because as soon as one of its financiers believes that an SSE-DFI is not viable he may lose interest and thus endanger the continuity of the institution as a whole. It is therefore important for all those involved to agree on a definition of viability. This will obviously depend on local conditions but one possible suggestion is: 'an SSE-DFI is viable if, based on its income-generating capacity and style and efficiency of its operations, it is able at least to break even when lending sums which have been attracted on a non-subsidized basis from the local and international capital market'. On this basis an SSE-DFI's viability is inversely proportional to the subsidies it needs.

This definition, if it is accepted, has important consequences for the future of SSE-DFIs, in quantitative and qualitative terms.

Quantitatively, the road to viability for SSE-DFI is a long one. The portfolio has to reach a minimum breakeven point before sufficient income can be generated to cover operating expenses and bad debt write-offs. A simple example makes it clear:

assumptions - operating expenditure: US$ 100,000 p.a.
           - bad debt write-offs: 3% of portfolio p.a.
           - 'spread': 10%

therefore - breakeven portfolio:

$$\frac{\$100,000}{(10\%-3\%)} \times 100 = \$1,500,000$$

If, more realistically, the spread is assumed to be 5 per cent, the breakeven portfolio rises to $ 5 million.

This example shows clearly that there will be an enormous pressure on the management of an SSE-DFI to minimize risks and operating expenditure and to maximize the size of the portfolio. This will inevitably lead to larger individual loans, of longer duration, and, in quantitative terms, the SSE-DFI will cease to be a development institution.

The response to this pressure will depend not only, or even mainly, on the figures, so much as on the motives and ambitions of the founders of the SSE-DFI in question. If the pressure for quantitative viability is tempered with a continuing awareness of the development role of the institution, the final results can be a viable institution which is also developmental. If the correct balance is not achieved, the SSE-DFI will cease to exist, devolve into a purely commercial institution with no developmental role, or become a permanent drain on local and foreign resources. The task, for founders, financiers and management, is not an easy one.

CONCLUSION

The FMO has placed great emphasis on the importance of creating viable institutions for small enterprise financing. SSE-DFIs may not be the ideal solution, nor the final answer. If a commercial bank, with a large branch network, is willing and able to provide short and long-term credit to small enterprises there is probably no need for an SSE-DFI, since it is very much a second best. In many countries, however, commercial banks are neither willing nor able to play this role and the SSE-DFI may be the best alternative.

It is uncertain whether SSE-DFIs will survive in the long run. If they are viable, commercial banks may pick up the challenge and the SSE-DFI will no longer be necessary. If, on the other hand, the SSE-DFI does not achieve viability and continually needs subsidy, the government will have to step in because the private institution has failed. In either case, the SSE-DFI may have only played a temporary role.

Much depends on the attitudes of the founders and financiers of the SSE-DFI. There are obvious tensions between noble objectives and viability; that is the choice between a charitable institution and a bank. The objective is to strike a balance between these two extremes while remaining viable.

Is it possible? In the end, the answer will depend on local savers and depositors on the local capital market, which must, automatically, be the long-term source of finance.

SMALL SCALE ENTERPRISES PROMOTION (SEP) LTD.

Mr. O.L.D. KAPIJIMPANGA
General Manager
SEP
Zambia

INTRODUCTION

Since 1977 the Zambian government has emphasized the need to promote small-scale enterprises, because they offer a possible long term solution to the problems of unemployment and rural underdevelopment. The Village Industry Service, a non-government organization, was founded in 1978 with support from the government to promote cottage and village industries, particularly in rural areas.

In 1981 the Small Industries Development Organization was established by the government to promote small enterprises and in 1982 the Development Bank of Zambia Act was amended in order to facilitate small enterprise financing through providing loans of up to 90 per cent of the total cost. There still remained the problem of equity; Small Scale Enterprises Promotion Ltd (SEP) was therefore established in order to complement the Development Bank of Zambia loans by equity participation or joint ventures.

In addition, a Credit Guarantee Scheme was drawn up and is now being ratified by Parliament. This is intended to reduce the risks and thus to make small enterprise lending more attractive to the commercial banks.

In general, small enterprise development has been considered from two points of view: promotion, which is mainly undertaken by Village Industry Service and the Small Industry Development Organization, and includes pre-investment studies, the wholesale supply of materials, industrial plots, transport and marketing; and finance, which is provided by the Development Bank of Zambia, commercial banks and SEP. The particular role of SEP is to facilitate loan demands by providing the necessary equity so that the small enterprises become bankable.

FINANCIAL ASSISTANCE

The central activity of SEP is the provision of equity to small enterprises through the formation of joint ventures; it is intended, in the future, that income from these investments should form the main source of income for SEP.

To date a total of US$ 90,000 has been committed to 14 client companies. The entrepreneurs themselves have contributed a further US$ 46,000 of their own funds, and as a result the 14 enterprises have been able to borrow a total of over half a million dollars in loans through the facility offered by the Development Bank of Zambia.

14

The actual disbursements of equity funds have amounted to date to US$ 54,000, from which a dividend of 12 per cent is ultimately expected. It is, however, unlikely that at this stage this figure will be realized and dividends from the equity investments are unlikely to be a significant source of revenue for SEP in its early years.

According to the terms of its investments, SEP is free after five years to dispose of its equity interest in its client companies. The entrepreneurs have first refusal of the shares, and it is hoped that they will take up the opportunity to increase their stakes in their own enterprises. They are encouraged to save money from their own salaries in the early years for this purpose.

SEP is not directly involved in the day-to-day management of its client companies but, through its having a nominee on their Board of Directors SEP is in close contact with their affairs. SEP's six staff meet on a regular weekly basis to discuss the fortunes of their clients and to recommend immediate and appropriate assistance if it appears to be necessary.

It is hoped that after SEP has been involved with an enterprise for five years it will have done sufficiently well for its shares to have reached the value which will provide a return to SEP. It is clear, however, that the growth of the client companies will depend on the quality of the other assistance which is offered to them to further operate efficiently in the Zambian market.

OTHER SERVICES

The experience of SEP over the past two years has shown that financial assistance alone, whether it is in loans or equity, is not sufficient. It is necessary to adopt an integrated approach.

In large companies, management problems are solved by various specialist departments and skilled employees. In a small business, the entrepreneur has to solve every problem himself. Zambian entrepreneurs generally lack the necessary accounting skills to find out whether their businesses are prospering or not. They have little or no bargaining power in buying raw materials or negotiating cash sales and are therefore often compelled to sell on 30 days or even longer credit. If technical problems arise, particularly those which could have been prevented through regular servicing, they lack the necessary skill to solve them themselves and cannot afford outside expertise. It is difficult to find reasonably priced premises and transport for raw materials and finished goods is generally unreliable and expensive. Because of all these problems, financial assistance alone is unlikely to be viable.

SEP have therefore found it necessary, in addition to finance, to provide management and accounting services, warehouse and transport, industrial estates, technical and marketing services and assistance in the preparation of pre-investment studies.

The management and accounting service involves introducing a simple accounting system into the client enterprise so that proper records are kept and management accounts can be drawn up and discussed with the entrepreneurs at the end of each month. This service is provided on site, and is reinforced by a series of seminars. The entrepreneurs pay a fee, ranging from US$ 20 - 120, depending on turnover and profit. As a result, SEP has adequate warning of forthcoming problems and the entrepreneurs themselves have a better understanding of their businesses.

Because of foreign exchange shortage, and the entrepreneurs' lack of working capital, raw material supplies are a major problem for small enterprises in Zambia. In addition, transport is not reliable and is expensive. SEP have therefore established a wholly owned subsidiary, MINTA, to provide warehousing and transport facilities. A total of US$ 50,000 has been invested in a warehouse, with initial stocks of 60 items and a truck which is available to client entrepreneurs for hire. MINTA is a viable enterprise in its own right; it purchases its materials from the cheapest possible source and resells them to entrepreneurs for a reasonable profit; it is planning to extend its activities to cover as many as possible of the entrepreneurs' requirements, within the financial resources that are available.

The Small Industry Development Organization has as yet been unable to address the problem of premises for small enterprises, and SEP has, as an intermediate measure, established its own Real Estate Company (SEPREC) to acquire, develop and rent or sell plots and sheds to small enterprises. An initial investment of US$ 114,000 has been made for a 12,000 sq m plot and it is planned to offer plots or sheds to at least 20 small enterprises. These will be provided either complete and ready to use, or with basic infrastructure and foundations only, together with the loan to enable the entrepreneur to finish the building in accordance with his own requirements.

SEP provides technical services by identifying and paying, through a grant from the Friedrich Ebert Foundation, local consultants for specific tasks. The client companies pay for the consultant's transport, in order to ensure that they have some commitment, but it is necessary to have a heavy degree of subsidy since the entrepreneurs cannot afford the full cost of technical expertise. The large parastatal retail outlets and other companies prefer to buy from the large well-established companies rather than from small enterprises. SEP acts as an informal intermediary, to ensure that these companies both place orders with client companies and settle their bills for cash or within a reasonable time. This credit is provided free of charge to SEP clients which have difficulties in disposing of their products.

SOURCES OF INCOME AND THE FUTURE OF SEP

SEP experience to date shows that the management and accounting services and the wholesale and transport services can provide a major source of income. The results for the eight months ending the 31 August 1985 show that SEP earned a substantial surplus over its operating expenses; the profit from wholesale and transport contributed 84 per cent of income, the fees for management and accounting services a further 11 per cent and the interest receivable only covered 5 per cent of income. As yet, no income has been received from the real estate subsidiary but it is possible that the return on this investment will be more than 30 per cent because of the shortage of premises for small enterprises in Lusaka.

It is interesting that in Lesotho BEDCO adopted a similar approach some years ago, but later found it necessary to withdraw from the equity participation, raw material supply and marketing operations, because they were not viable. It is hoped that SEP will be more successful.

In addition to the rather larger equity investments which have already been referred to, it has also been found that many small enterprises require very small loans for working capital or fixed investments in order to make them viable. The commercial banking sector has not responded to this need and SEP has therefore recently established a small fund of US$ 25,000 for this purpose. Loans of up to a maximum of US$ 2,500 each for a period of up to 18 months at 17.5 per cent interest rate will be made from this fund. So far some US$ 7,500 of loans have been approved and US$ 5,000 have been disbursed. It is, at this stage, too early to assess the success of this programme.

SEP is currently being registered as a financial institution with the government. When this has been completed, SEP will be a fullfledged SSE-DFI, authorized to provide both equity and loan funds. SEP will then shift its major emphasis away from equity to loan financing.

At this point, the rate of interest will therefore be of vital concern for the viability of SEP.

Interest on loans to small enterprises is a political issue in Zambia since the government prefers to offer lower rates to small enterprises than to other borrowers. The Development Bank of Zambia and other agencies have opted to lend to small enterprises at three per cent below the normal lending rate, and it can be expected that this differential rate will remain in force for the next two years.

Loans made by SEP to its own subsidiaries, however, such as the wholesale and transport service or the real estate company, clearly do not require any concessional rate of interest and these companies could in fact afford to pay higher than the market rate. If SEP retains its ownership, however, any benefit from low interest loans to these subsidiaries will be expressed in higher dividends from its equity investment and the curtailment of interest rates, if it is applied to such loans, need therefore cause no problems. This emphasizes, once more, the profit potential of small enterprise services, which can both assist SEP's clients and also provide a source of income for SEP itself. It is important, however, to be aware of the extent to which such profits depend on SEP's privileged access to foreign exchange or other cash resources. If SEP is to be a genuinely viable SSE-DFI, it must not rely on such privileged access, and this may mean that in the future SEP will have to rely more on dividends and capital gains from its equity investments than on profits earned by providing other services to its client enterprises.

Although SEP is at an early stage in its development, it demonstrates one approach whereby financial services can be integrated with the other services which are necessary to eliminate the constraints which confront its small enterprise clients. This approach not only reduces the risk of the investments, but can also provide an important source of income for the institution itself.

SMALL ENTERPRISES FINANCING ORGANIZATION (SEFO) INC.

Mr. R.M. MORRIS
Managing Director
SEFO
Liberia

SMALL ENTERPRISES IN LIBERIA

The small enterprise sector in Liberia suffers from a number of constraints and is as yet poorly developed. The economy is highly dualistic: a large traditional agricultural sector co-exists with a number of foreign-controlled extractive and plantation industries, which account for 70 per cent of export earnings and a substantial proportion of the economy as a whole. Apart from the above enclave industries, the manufacturing sector is small, mainly involved in import substitution and largely foreign owned and managed; it contributes only one per cent of total exports. Most Liberian manufacturers produce consumer goods for standard international tastes and the high income market, using capital intensive techniques. The skewed income distribution favours the growth of such production and the government's industrial policies have provided further impetus in this direction.

Small enterprises, defined as firms with assets up to US$ 50,000, offer a full range of basic economic activities to a large and poor section of the economy. Despite this, they are largely unrecognized and unregulated. Most small enterprises are in Monrovia with a small proportion in other parts of the country. A 1980 survey counted 7000 units; the largest number was tailors, restaurants, carpenters, transport businesses and garages. According to this survey the enterprises had few fixed assets, they suffered from intense competition, they lacked utilities, had limited space and distinctly distrusted government and banking bureaucracy. The entrepreneurs are not good managers and are only at best vaguely aware of how they may expand their business or improve their efficiency.

Any attempt to develop small enterprises is constrained because adult literacy is only 30 per cent and the economy is basically agricultural. Most Liberian small-scale business people belong to the lowest socio-economic group. In addition, they suffer from all the pressures of a traditional society: a successful entrepreneur, in addition to his business, has to meet all the normal requirements of his extended family.

In addition to this, the entrepreneur suffers from pressures and threats from petty officials and others. Lending experience to date confirms the pressures; loan repayments are often not made because of family needs such as burials, school fees, personal debts and child birth. In addition, the entrepreneurs often have to leave their businesses because of social commitments and this creates still further problems.

Traditionally, Liberians left commerce in the hands of expatriates. There had been no tradition for the growth of indigenous entrepreneurship. Such entrepreneurs as there are, are largely imitators, rather than innovators, preferring to engage in retailing rather than manufacturing. This has been attributed to the educational system which is directed towards government and large foreign companies, with very little relevance to small business. The civil service, the professions and politics enjoy greater prestige than business. Liberian entrepreneurs are often informal part-time managers, being employed by government or large businesses at the same time.

Because of these factors, and because entrepreneurs mistrust institutions, it is very difficult to build any type of assistance agencies. Nevertheless, small enterprises seem to be the most appropriate way of involving more Liberians in the economy which is at present very much controlled by foreigners. Small enterprises are labour intensive and the scale of their production matches the limited local market. The sector's growth has been retarded because of lack of private and public support. The government has yet to introduce policies to encourage sub-contracting by large enterprises to small ones, or by providing appropriate incentives to small business.

THE LIBERIAN BANKING SECTOR

The banks in Liberia are largely foreign owned; they are biased towards large foreign owned businesses and play a limited role in indigenous development. Four of the ten banks are Liberian owned but the foreign banks have the major share of the market. The Liberian Bank for Development and Investment (LBDI) and The Agricultural Credit and Development Bank (ACDB) do provide some finance to Liberian owned businesses, but they have limited resources and other priorities. They have made few non-agricultural small enterprise loans. The commercial banks concentrate on trade financing, credit to public corporations and to plantations. The manufacturing sector only has 5.7 per cent of total credit, and most of this is for short term requirements of foreign owned businesses.

The banks themselves are beset by many problems. They have inadequate cash for domestic needs and to satisfy external obligations; they are affected by declining export revenues and increased legal reserve requirements and because of cheque clearing problems there are heavy demands for cash for business dealings. This makes the control of small enterprise loans very complicated. The growing budget deficit makes problems even worse, and because Liberia uses the US dollar as its currency there is a severe drain of capital abroad in times of uncertainty.

Regardless of its present problems, the banks have never been receptive to the needs of small businesses. Entrepreneurs

20

cannot present bankable proposals, they lack collateral and they are poor managers; they are therefore considered bad risks. Funds provided by the National Bank of Liberia and The World Bank were not fully used, because of the reluctance of the commercial banks to lend to this sector.

THE BEGINNING OF SEFO

In 1980, the government started to give some priority to small enterprises. The small and medium business department was set up within the newly established National Investment Commission and the Ministry of Planning and Economic Affairs decided to offer assistance to small enterprises. It was clear that there was a need for a package of services for small enterprises, to provide linkages with the public enterprise sector and to promote the use of local raw materials.

The World Bank/National Bank of Liberia Programme was designed to provide long-term loans to manufacturing enterprises, administered through the commercial banks. The SEFO programme was designed to offer a wider range of assistance, including leasing, equity financing and long and short-term loans, for enterprises in the Monrovia industrial estate or elsewhere, and this was formally accepted by the government of Liberia during 1980/81.

The priority area for SEFO was the woodworking sector, but the proposal also allowed the inclusion of tailors, builders and other types of enterprise in Monrovia and the neighbouring county. It was envisaged that other areas would be included once SEFO had the necessary financial resources.

It was recognized from the outset that technical assistance and business advice was required as well as finance; borrowers under the National Bank of Liberia Programme were to receive assistance from the small and medium business department of the National Investment Commission, while Partnership for Productivity Liberia, a voluntary regional developmental association, was to provide business advice to SEFO clients in Nimba.

SEFO was formally registered in August 1981; FMO provided two long-term advisors to assist in building the institution and providing technical advice. The management was totally Liberian and Liberian institutions provided the equity, while the major finance came in the form of loans in equal proportions from the Liberian Bank for Development and Investment (LBDI) and FMO.

THE VIABILITY OF SEFO DURING ITS EARLY YEARS

It had been originally planned that SEFO should at first use LBDI's staff and facilities when its portfolio was insufficient to cover the overheads involved in hiring its own staff. This approach did not involve sufficient commitment to small enterprise lending, however, and a separate institution was soon developed with its own staff. The only linkage with the LBDI during this period was for advice on legal aspects, loan procedures and loan evaluation in sectors where LBDI had experience.

From the beginning SEFO's management was primarily concerned to ensure its viability. This was not easy because of the sluggish condition of the economy, lack of experience, entrepreneurial weakness and SEFO's own weak financial base because of its high costs of borrowings and the necessarily high transaction cost.

In spite of the economy's export revenue problems, the small enterprise sector relies mainly on the domestic market and is thus performing relatively well. It was estimated at the end of June 1985 that SEFO's clients only included some ten per cent of the potential businesses in manufacturing, construction and service industries. The problem, in fact, is not the depressed economy or the lack of opportunities but the shortage of good ideas and effective entrepreneurs. The low number of applications that reach the stage of formal appraisal confirms that there is a scarcity of entrepreneurs with sufficient judgement, initiative, courage and determination to conceive and launch individual enterprises, and of managers to run these enterprises successfully. Because of this, there are not enough good proposals, the loan portfolio is of a low quality and the debt recovery rate is poor.

It follows, therefore, that advisory services must be a vital element in SEFO's viability. This task was in SEFO's original design assigned to the National Investment Commission and Partnership for Productivity. These institutions, however, have their own programmes and obligations; differences of emphasis emerged which while not prohibiting cooperation, meant that SEFO's clients did not receive the extensive service they needed. Effective non-financial support was not provided to SEFO's clients and potential clients, either at the stage of project development or once they were in business. The high provision for bad debts during SEFO's early years demonstrates this deficiency.

SEFO's final problem was funding. Given its structure, its cost of capital and the high set-up cost, SEFO was unlikely to achieve viability in a reasonable time without drastically changing its financial structure. SEFO was designed to be an independent institution complete with its own administration. Salaries and wages, staff training, pre-loan advice to applicants and the time management had to spend in complying with the complicated pre-disbursement procedures required by SEFO'S funding agencies involved high expenditures. At the end of the pre-operating period, expenditures amounted to a total of US$ 265,624. The initial capital was not sufficient to cover these costs along with continuing deficits. In addition, two of the Liberian shareholders were unable to take up their allotted shares.

In these circumstances, loan funds became the crucial element in SEFO's survival. In 1983 SEFO's weighted cost of capital was 10.4 per cent, giving a spread of about eight per cent. The cost of funds for lending and operations was very high in relation to SEFO's earnings, and interest charges alone in 1983 came to over 80 per cent of gross income from loans and interest on undisbursed funds.

The following data, which are based on SEFO's audited accounts for 1984, give some indication of the position:

average loan portfolio	US$662,045
operating cost as a percentage of above portfolio	59%
financial charges as a percentage of above portfolio .	14%
provision for bad debts	20%
cost of funds loaned	73%
interest earned	18%
other income	9%
gross negative spread	46%
(before provision for bad debts)	
government grant	3%
net negative spread	43%

The above shows that the government grant is inadequate and must be increased substantially until such time as SEFO can achieve viability. In other countries, loans to small enterprises are highly subsidized either directly by government or by cross-subsidy from earnings on loans to larger enterprises; SEFO existed without support from either source. The Liberian Bank for Development and Investment charged 15.5 per cent on the funds lent to SEFO, and in 1982, in order to cover its operating cost, SEFO had to issue US$ 200,000 worth of 12 per cent debentures to two local banks in order to cover its losses.

A NEW APPROACH TO VIABILITY

SEFO was now in some difficulty, because of inadequate initial funding, continuing operating deficits and ineffective pre- and post-loan client assistance. In conjunction with donors, management developed a plan to enable SEFO to achieve viability by 1988/89. Two vital needs had to be addressed simultaneously. The immediate priority was to attract soft loans to on-lend to small enterprises and capital to finance operating deficits. Secondly, the quality of the loan portfolio had to be improved through better loan administration and closer control over advisory services to SEFO's existing and potential clients.

The financial plan showed that the weighted cost of capital would have to be 3.8 per cent and the loan portfolio to total US$ 4 million in order for SEFO to break even. USAID was the first institution to be interested in this proposal and a more detailed design was drawn up incorporating non-financial services.

The plan made the following assumptions relating to SEFO's viability:
- average cost of new soft loan funds for on-lending 2.5%
- soft loans from external sources 1984/89 ....   US$ 5M.
- target loan portfolio by end of 1989 .... 300-400 SSE loans for approximately US$ 5.5M. (net of US$ 1.5M. cumulative write-down for bad and doubtful debts).

The forecast statement of operations was as follows:
- gross income   .... US$ 1.3 million
- less operating cost   .... US$ 0.5 million
- finance charges   .... US$ 200,000
- provision for losses   .... US$ 300,000
- total expenses   .... US$ 1 million
- net income   .... US$ 300,000

Although this plan was based on a projection of steadily increasing loan recoveries, it should be noted that even by 1989 the forecast of losses of principal alone, of US$ 300,000, was still equal to 60 per cent of operating expenses. Further, if gross income was based on a portfolio before write-downs, income would rise to US$ 1.65 million. By computing a gross income of US$ 1.3 million on the written down portfolio, there is a further 'hidden' cost provision of US$ 350,000. If this is added to the 'open' provision for write-downs of US$ 300,000, the total write-downs come to US$ 650,000 which is considerably more than three times the financial charges.

A further hidden cost factor in these forecasts is the cost of business advisory services, providing pre-loan services to SEFO clients. Foreign assistance covered not only expatriate staff salary and associated overheads of US$ 480,000, but also local cost of US$ 152,000. This latter cost would have to be absorbed by SEFO when foreign assistance was withdrawn and this would make the total cost even higher. This graphically illustrates the true cost of lending to risky small enterprises.

In the plan, operating expenses were projected to rise five per cent per year, implying a rapid increase in efficiency since the portfolio was forecast to rise from US$ 1 million to US$ 4 million. Operating deficits were predicted to continue, and the plan provided for US$ 750,000 capital grant to cover these, supported by long-term financial advice to assist SEFO in the implementation of the programme.

It was also proposed to establish technical and business assistance services to SEFO clients, which SEFO would directly control. This was just as important as the plan for financial assistance, since without such non-financial services it would be impossible to achieve the great expansion in the portfolio and increased loan recoveries on which viability depended.

It was proposed to establish a Business Advisory Service (BAS), sharing offices and working closely with SEFO on a day-to-day basis to service clients. The BAS was initially to be autonomous and separately funded, but after the first five years some of its functions were to be integrated into SEFO's operations by which time it should be financially feasible.

This innovative programme was approved by USAID in mid-1984. Shortly thereafter, a Senior Financial Advisor started work, and BAS was established. The initial task of BAS, which was to be achieved during 1984, was to recruit and train its field advisory staff. BAS could then start operations, including marketing and business development aimed at attracting potential borrowers, working with them to identify or more closely specify their ideas and loan needs, and advising and monitoring the progress of borrowers' businesses.

BAS covers the basic business functions of marketing, accounting, production and general management, with both potential and operating businesses. It is also planned to strengthen assistance in the field of appropriate technology. It is too early to judge how effective the BAS experiment is, but the prospects are favourable; because SEFO is close to BAS they have been able to influence the type of clients which are serviced and the appropriate emphasis on the various non-financial functions.

Clients appear to benefit from book-keeping and cost-control systems and new perspectives for marketing. BAS has had a special impact on the success of poultry and pig farms, where they have specialist technical assistance, and it is hoped that this level of technical assistance will in future be available in other sectors. It is too early to quantify the impact of BAS, beyond the favourable prospects and good working relationship which have so far been established. The direct impact of the capital grant can however be more easily quantified. The expensive LBDI loan has been retired and the average cost of capital has been reduced to five per cent from the figure of over 10 per cent in 1983-84. SEFO has also requested that the interest charged on funds borrowed from NBL/IDA Programme should be reduced from 10.5 per cent to 2.5 per cent.

SEFO's financial position has been further improved through new grant, equity and soft loan funds since the new approach to viability has been introduced. Loan appraisals have been tightened up and the collections are undertaken by SEFO's own staff in the field. Demand notes are issued by computer, thanks to BAS assistance and, by combining offices with BAS, SEFO's overheads have been reduced, so that rents and utility costs, for instance, have been reduced by one third.

The UNIDO Small and Medium Enterprises Development Support Programme at the NIC is directly linked with SEFO, through UNIDO's funding of a full-time adviser on project analysis and supervision.

All the efforts made so far have generated positive results. The cost of capital has been reduced, new capital has been attracted, the internal organization has been improved and BAS technical assistance is being provided. The efficiency of collection has improved by 50 per cent in early 1985 over 1984, but there has not been time for the improvement in loan appraisal and administration to be reflected in increased collection efficiency on new loans, nor is the efficiency of collection on the entire portfolio yet satisfactory.

As for the prospect of increasing the loan portfolio to US$ 4 million, both the European Community and the German DEG are interested in SEFO's rural enterprise activities. The EC have asked to finance the rehabilitation of small rubber farms, through grant funds, and they are also considering providing soft loan funds to finance rural enterprises in Bong and Lofa counties. The DEG is considering investing in both equity and loans.

The internal organization of SEFO has been improved; it is a small organization and its board members play a substantial part in its management. The emphasis on lending has gradually been shifted to productive enterprises in order to promote employment and increase value added. Loan applications are more rigorously screened, with more emphasis on client ability and integrity, and intensive efforts are being made to improve the efficiency of collections. Although some policy changes have been made to allow for the peculiarities of the small enterprise sector, improvements are still needed in the requirements for client equity, collateral and documentation.

In addition, some loss making enterprises have been revived, thus improving the portfolio, enhancing entrepreneur's confidence in SEFO and providing valuable lessons for future project appraisals. It is difficult to quantify the results of these improvements, but there are signs of progress and prospects are favourable.

A DEVELOPING MODEL: THE LIBERIAN EXPERIENCE

The following conclusions, from SEFO's experience of initiating small enterprise lending in Liberia, may be useful in the design of similar programmes elsewhere:

a) The high risks of small enterprise lending in Liberia prevented the larger banks from lending to small enterprises, so that it was necessary to set up an independent organization, with high and non-recoverable start-up costs and no experience. SEFO has not been able to cross-subsidize small enterprise loans with the returns on larger ones, nor has substantial government subsidy been available. Low-cost loan funds and adequate initial capital support to cover start-up costs and operating deficits were therefore crucial to SEFO's survival.

b) Given the weakness of the small enterprise sector, however, loans and availability of capital for on-lending are not enough for the viability of the lending institution or the healthy growth of its clients. Complementary non-financial services are needed both by the small enterprises and by the lending institution in order to ensure its viability.

c) It is essential that non-financial business services and technical advice should be provided at all stages, in close collaboration with the financial institution, otherwise intolerably bad debts will result. When effective non-financial services are unavailable, one approach is to set up an autonomous, separately funded body to fill the gap, with a specific mandate to service the financial institution's potential and existing clients.

Later, as the lending institution achieves a sound and viable portfolio, some of the non-financial functions can be taken into its operations, while others, particularly project promotion and technical services, may be dedicated to private consultancies, government agencies and independent non-financial institutions.

FOREIGN DONORS AND LOCAL FUNDS FOR SSE-DFI FINANCE

Mr. ASWIN KONGSIRI
Senior Executive Vice President
The Industrial Finance Corporation of Thailand (IFCT)
Thailand

INTRODUCTION

The IFCT opened its small industry financing window in April 1984 and took over the management of the Small Industry Credit Guarantee Fund on its establishment in May 1985. Although IFCT had been closely involved in the preparation of both these activities for several years beforehand, small business is only a very small, although rapidly growing, proportion of IFCT's total operations.

By June 1985 116 projects had been approved for a total of approximately US$ 12 million. The objective is to achieve additionality, and although some small-scale clients may qualify for credit from commercial banks, they may prefer IFCT because of its particular terms.

IFCT has separate departments for project appraisal and supervision of large investments; this is not the case for small enterprises, and the same office that prepares the project document is also responsible for follow-up. This is done deliberately because IFCT believes that a personal relationship between the entrepreneurs and the project officers is of great importance. In pursuance of this policy, every small-scale client is visited at least twice a year, and as more branches are established even more frequent contact will become possible.

Most small-scale clients necessarily have commercial banking relationships, since IFCT provides only long-term investment and permanent working capital credit. IFCT was instrumental in the establishment of the credit guarantee scheme because so many small-scale applications had to be rejected because of the lack of collateral. In the long term, commercial banks may follow IFCT's example and, because of their branch network and their local currency resources, they are in a better position than IFCT to provide credit to small industries. In addition, the Credit Guarantee Fund both informs and reassures the commercial banks, and their future involvement may have important consequences for IFCT's own funds.

IFCT controls the costs of small enterprise financing closely, in order to be able to calculate whether the activity will be self-sustaining in the future. The level of bad debts is the key indicator, but it is at this time too early to forecast what this will be. In IFCT's view, viability means a positive return on investment. Should it appear that small enterprise lending is not viable when separately costed, IFCT will wind down the operation.

Ideally, SSE-DFIs should use only domestic resources, since most small enterprise financing needs are in local currency. It is, however, well-known that DFIs of all kinds find it difficult to raise sufficient local funds to meet their requirements. It is important they examine why there are limits to the use of local funds, and why foreign donors have a role to play in what appears at first sight to be essentially a local currency operation.

BARRIERS TO THE USE OF LOCAL FUNDS

Equity

Share capital is of course the first source of local currency for an SSE-DFI. If the institution is profitable and does not have to pay out large dividends, as is the case of most government sponsored institutions, then the original equity plus retained earnings can be a significant source of local currency funds for on-lending. The proportion of funds available from this source, however, will be affected by the debt-equity ratio policy of the institution. The higher the ratio of debt to equity, the lower the percentage of funds from equity.

Governments are severely limited in their ability to allocate scarce funds to the capital of DFIs. In most developing countries capital markets are either underdeveloped or non-existent, and in any case SSE-DFIs are not particularly profitable.

It may be possible to persuade other financial institutions to invest in the equity of SSE-DFIs but this cannot be considered desirable. It can only, perhaps, be justified if the sound expansion of an SSE-DFI is constrained by shortage of equity. Foreign donors can assist by investing in the equity of SSE-DFIs, and many have done so. An additional advantage, apart from the funds themselves, is that this enables the foreign donor to have a role in the management of the institution. The percentage of foreign shares will be limited for obvious reasons, and may not be possible at all in some cases, although some foreign donors may be allowed temporary local shareholder status.

Over the longer term, foreign donors can play an important role by assisting in the development of local capital markets and by persuading SSE-DFIs to raise at least some of their equity from local sources. This can be beneficial, since the SSE-DFI will then have a market based indicator of its financial efficiency, as well as broadening its source of funding.

IFCT operates at the low debt equity ratio of under five to one, although the ceiling imposed by its creditors is eight to one. Since small enterprise lending is still only a small percentage of total assets, IFCT's equity far exceeds the small industry financing requirements which could theoretically thus be funded solely from share capital.

IFCT prefers, however, to maximize its use of foreign donor resources for small enterprise lending; this can be justified on macro-economic grounds, as large quantities of local currency are required for medium and larger projects and IFCT's shares are listed in the stock market and new capital issues are made regularly. It is thus necessary to pay a reasonable dividend and local equity is thus expensive when compared to foreign donor funds.

In addition, some 38 per cent of IFCT's share capital is held by foreign shareholders, most of which are financial institutions. Foreign ownership is limited by law to a maximum of 49 per cent.

Deposits

Deposits can be an important source of local currency funds for short-term and working capital SSE finance, but most SSE-DFIs lack the deposit-taking capacity of commercial banks. Since deposits require an elaborate and expensive branch network, this is not usually a viable source of funds for SSE-DFIs. It is important, however, for an SSE-DFI to have access to local currency to meet its clients' working capital needs. This can be done by linking with the commercial banking system or by obtaining a line of credit from government or the central bank, in order to conserve long-term funds for fixed assets financing.

Bonds and debentures

The most appropriate way for an SSE-DFI to mobilize local currency for long-term lending is through issuing medium or long-term bonds or debentures in the domestic capital market. There are many obstacles, however, which limit this source of funds.

Domestic capital markets are usually not sufficiently developed to accept securities with maturities of more than two or three years. There are few if any interest rate differentials between short and long-term bonds, and even if some long-term funds are available, as statutorily required for financial institutions or for insurance companies, they are often granted to government for its own domestic borrowing needs. The SSE-DFIs have to offer sufficiently high rates of interest on their bonds to compete with short-term investments and government bonds. This usually makes bonds a prohibitively expensive source of funding.

It is equally important to develop local capital markets for bonds and debentures as for shares. Nevertheless, it is still not clear that SSE-DFIs can fund themselves solely from capital market sources, given the high spread which they need. If long term commercial funds can be blended with concessional funds, this can greatly expand the resource base of an SSE-DFI.

Government assistance

Because of the above constraints, all SSE-DFIs have to some extent to depend on government help in obtaining long-term local currency. This can be provided in the form of a direct grant which can be added to equity, can be used to subsidize interest rates or for technical assistance such as training programmes, entrepreneurship development or extension. Rediscounting or direct loans can be made available on concessional terms and blended with funds from the capital market. Government guarantees for bonds and debentures can provide the institution with better access to the limited long-term domestic capital market, and tax exemptions can also enhance its ability to raise long-term funds.

There is, however, a limit on the amount of assistance that government can provide, especially on concessional terms, although guarantees and tax exemptions do not entail actual cash allocations and are thus less constrained. It can be concluded, therefore, that SSE-DFIs cannot rely solely on domestic capital markets nor on direct government assistance and that they must therefore turn to foreign sources to support their operations.

SOURCES OF FOREIGN CURRENCY AND THEIR LIMITS

There are numerous sources of foreign currency which are available for SSE-DFIs, and management must keep track of developments in order to optimize their institution's resource base. The sources vary from highly concessional to purely commercial. Every SSE-DFI will obviously want to maximize its use of concessional sources. It is also generally true, however, that the more concessional the funds, the more conditions are attached to them, although some multilateral agencies have recently continued to impose restrictive conditions while charging near to commercial rates of interest.

Every donor institution has its own reasons for determining the terms and conditions on which it provides funds; similarly, every SSE-DFI has its own policies with regard to the funds it uses. It is also natural that the more concessional the funds or the more desperate the SSE-DFI, the greater the 'leverage' the donor has over its client. It is important that this leverage should be used with restraint.

Foreign exchange is necessary to augment scarce or expensive domestic currency, but this does not mean that foreign exchange can be used without limits. The World Bank and the Asian Development Bank have for many years debated the amount of local currency expenditure that can be financed with their loans. Operation manuals usually stipulate that foreign loans can only be used to finance direct and indirect foreign currency expenditures. The Asian Development Bank has even imposed a limit on the proportion of its loans which can be used for indirect foreign exchange expenditures and at the same time the bank expects that a higher proportion of its loans should be on-lent to small businesses.

Since most small enterprises use locally made or at least locally assembled equipment, and SSE-DFIs are always under pressure to minimize their transaction cost, it is important that they are not burdened with the heavy administrative costs of estimating the indirect foreign exchange cost involved in different types of investments. Fortunately, most donors are aware of this problem and are much more flexible about how their loans are used for local currency expenditures. Donors are nevertheless correct to insist that a part of an SSE-DFI's funds should come from domestic sources. Since foreign loans obtained by most SSE-DFIs need some form of government support, they are a part of the government foreign borrowing programme and must accordingly be subject to the limits imposed by the country's ability to service its international debt. The prudence of the country's overall policy may be questioned, and donors should indeed be concerned with this, but it is too restrictive to impose strict limits on individual SSE-DFIs.

One useful indicator of whether an SSE-DFI is relying excessively on foreign loans is to estimate the actual foreign exchange earnings and savings generated by its clients and to compare these with its foreign debt service payments. Foreign exchange earnings of course fluctuate from year to year, and foreign exchange savings should be calculated to include only the savings in real terms, but if such an approximate estimate totals a much lower amount than the foreign debt servicing requirements of the SSE-DFI, this indicates that the foreign borrowing programme is having an unfavourable impact on the country's external debt position. The government would in such a case have to compare these costs with the other economic and social benefits which are being achieved by the small enterprise lending programme.

FOREIGN EXCHANGE RISK

The foreign exchange risk is a more specific factor which affects the amount of foreign borrowing which can be undertaken by an SSE-DFI. It is generally accepted that this risk should not be passed on to the small enterprise borrowers, and some donors in fact make this a condition of their loans. At the same time, most authorities on financial management of development finance institutions state categorically that these institutions should not bear the foreign exchange risk themselves, and this tenet is often enshrined in their policy statements.

In countries with extremely high rates of inflation and constant devaluations, there is no choice but to pass on the foreign exchange risk to borrowers, in which case it is vital to evaluate carefully their ability to absorb the risk, by export sales or in other ways. In such circumstances the use of foreign exchange will be severely constrained, and it becomes even more important to mobilize domestic resources.

In more normal circumstances the SSE-DFI still needs some support from government. The easiest way is for the government to borrow the foreign exchange and to lend the proceeds to the SSE-DFI in local currency. Many government-owned SSE-DFIs serve merely as lending and collection agencies for their own governments, and do not have the responsibility of raising their own resources. It is suggested, however, that it is impossible to divorce the mobilization of the sources from their allocations. If this separation is made, hidden or unacknowledged subsidies will result and will impair the ability of the SSE-DFI to contribute to long-term viability of small businesses. If the government takes the foreign exchange risk on behalf of the SSE-DFI, even if a spread is added to cover this risk, which is rarely done, the danger is that the cost of funds will be underestimated and thus capital will be underpriced.

One solution to this typical problem is a mechanism by which the SSE-DFI bears the foreign exchange risk itself but is protected against any liquidity problems that might arise from the risk by a special funding agreement with government. IFCT uses such a mechanism and it has worked well, with some amendments, for the past 12 years. For each foreign currency borrowed by IFCT, a foreign exchange risk fee is negotiated between the institution and the government. The amount is determined by an assessment of the trend of the value of the foreign currency relative to the Thai baht, the rate of interest compared to IFCT's on-lending rate, and the size of the foreign exchange risk reserve fund when compared with IFCT's total foreign exposure. The fee, which is considered part of IFCT's cost of funds, is paid into the reserve fund to cover the foreign exchange risk.

If a foreign exchange loss is actually incurred, IFCT can draw on the fund to cover the loss. If, however, the fund is insufficient, government will advance funds to cover the shortfall. IFCT has to repay such advances at a rate of about US$ 110,000 per annum, or 3 per cent of the net profit, whichever is higher. If a foreign exchange profit is made, this has to be paid into the reserve fund.

This mechanism forces IFCT to be aware of the true cost of foreign currency, and the cost is adjusted to meet changing economic conditions. IFCT has to manage its foreign exchange resources prudently, and has an incentive to use all the financial techniques available, such as currency swaps and options, forward markets and so on, to minimize its risk. More importantly, there is a strong incentive for IFCT to mobilize domestic currency resources whenever possible. Nevertheless, this mechanism has caused disagreement between the World Bank and IFCT over how unrealized foreign exchange losses should be treated in the institution's financial statements.

Multilateral lending institutions have given SSE-DFIs little assistance in the area of foreign exchange risk, beyond suggesting that the government should bear this risk on behalf of the institution. This may be why multilateral lenders have tended over the past decade to floating exchange rates to lend more to government-owned institutions where the government finds it easier to accept the risk. Other bilateral donors have been more flexible and have lowered the interest rates not only to accommodate the higher spread needed for lending to small businesses, but also to allow some coverage of the foreign exchange risk. Other matters such as variable maturity loans are being explored, but the main principle should not be forgotten: the real cost of foreign borrowing must be recognized and should be reflected in the cost of loans made to small businesses.

It is important also to recognize one other aspect of foreign exchange risk which is specific to multilateral lending institutions. They can disburse their loans in any currency they wish, and this may be completely different from the currency of procurement or the currency which the borrower wants as part of its foreign exchange risk. It would be of considerable assistance if multilateral lenders were more sympathetic to the SSE-DFIs' problems when they allocate their currencies and when they give notice of repayment, so that the institutions can plan their foreign currency exposures more efectively and take advantage of hedging techniques.

THE COST OF FUNDS AND MATURITIES

It has already been pointed out that the long-term funds in local currency, if available at all, are generally more expensive than foreign currency. If foreign exchange risk is also taken into account, the effective cost of funds from home and abroad should come closer, but in developing countries this usually applies only to short-term funds since domestic long-term funds are very scarce.

Furthermore, SSE-DFIs usually have access to concessional sources of foreign funds, such as donor institutions. There is therefore a natural tendency for these institutions to maximize their foreign borrowing in order to reduce their average cost of funds. The dangers inherent in this policy in terms of foreign exchange risks and the effect on the country's external debt position have already been mentioned. If these factors are properly taken into account, a carefully calculated blend of concessional, commercial and domestic funds can enable an SSE-DFI to have a sufficient spread for its operations while maintaining its own interest rates at close to the prime lending rate, or at a rate which is low enough to encourage small enterprises to go through the bureaucratic processes required by SSE-DFIs.

As it is usually difficult or expensive for an SSE-DFI to raise domestic currency loans with a maturity of over three years, while the maturity of their on-lending to small enterprises is on average about five years, it is important for these institutions to obtain longer maturities on their foreign loans in order to avoid cash flow and debt servicing problems. Foreign donors, by providing longer maturities, can therefore enable SSE-DFIs to extend longer maturities to their borrowers and to mobilize more domestic resources.

INTEREST RATES AND TYPES OF CAPITAL AVAILABLE TO SMALL ENTERPRISES

It is important that an SSE-DFI should lend long-term funds at a fixed rate of interest in order to provide their clients with one element of certainty in their cost structure. If a floating rate based on some overseas benchmark is used, it is difficult for the small-scale borrower to understand, let alone to predict, the change in his financing cost. A variable rate may be acceptable for short-term working capital, but this should be based on domestic interest rates. It is therefore necessary for foreign donors to lend to SSE-DFIs at fixed rates of interest, since the uncertainties of the foreign exchange risk are serious enough without the additional concern of fluctuating interest rates.

Some foreign donors require SSE-DFIs to consult them before changing their on-lending rates. Since the interest rate of an SSE-DFI is the most critical factor in its viability as a financial institution and its role in promoting viable clients, donors have an important contribution to make in providing advice in this area, as long as they remember the political and economic environment in which the institution has to operate. All the critical factors, namely the availability and cost of domestic resources, the extent of foreign borrowing, the foreign exchange risk and the operating spread, come together to determine the lending rates. If any of these factors are overlooked or underestimated, or if the SSE-DFI is tempted to reduce interest rates for purely political reasons, its viability will be undermined. An outside institution can often provide the objectivity necessary to perceive and to point out potential dangers.

The shortage of equity has been a chronic and critical problem for small enterprise financing. In many cases the entrepreneur's equity is financed by loans from relatives and friends, or from money-lenders. Given the family nature of many small businesses, however, it may not be possible for an SSE-DFI to provide equity financing, but when it is possible institutions should not be constrained by the lack of funds. This is of course a high risk area requiring careful appraisal and follow-up. Donor institutions such as the Asian Development Bank have recently become interested in providing lines for equity financing to development finance institutions and commercial banks under which the institution also has to make an equal equity investment from its own funds. If the terms and conditions are appropriate, such facilities should stimulate SSE-DFIs into becoming more active in equity financing, although the projects covered by the Asian Development Bank in this way are medium rather than small-scale.

SSE-DFIs can also provide equity financing through venture capital funds. The International Finance Corporation has already supported such a scheme for countries in South-East Asia, although this is again designed more for medium-sized projects. The IFCT is exploring the possibility of setting up a venture capital fund for small agro-industry production in Thailand, where the potential for low cost technological break-throughs is very great. Foreign donors can make a major contribution by making joint investment in such schemes with SSE-DFIs.

Together with equity and long-term loans, working capital is one of the three critical components of SSE funding. Working capital should be financed in local currency, but in view of the constraints mentioned above, foreign donors should allow some of their loans to be used to finance working capital, without limiting this to indirect foreign exchange requirements. In particular permanent working capital can be financed by foreign loans within the limits of foreign borrowing which were outlined earlier. Foreign donors should in any event not provide all the working capital and should ensure that an SSE-DFI has the means to provide adequate working capital in financing itself or that it is available through other domestic institutions.

NON-FINANCIAL ASPECTS

Foreign donors can play an important negative or positive role in the non-financial aspects of an SSE-DFI's operation. Technical assistance for extension services and training is important, and donors can provide grants for this purpose to ease the pressure on the SSE-DFI's spread although part of the cost should be borne by the borrower itself. IFCT has been encouraged to undertake such non-financial activities, for instance, by the system whereby part of the interest differential in capital aid loans from KFW to IFCT is paid into a counterpart fund which can be used for extension service, training and promotion. In providing technical assistance, however, donors should encourage the use of local expertise and should not restrict the use of funds to foreign exchange expenditures only. The IFCT, for instance, uses its own subsidiary, the Industrial Management Company, for technical services.

Multilateral donors have in the past paid a great deal of attention to institution building and policy advice, but as the development finance institutions have evolved over the past ten years, there is need for caution in performing this role. It is important for donors not to impose their own ideas on SSE-DFIs without a thorough assessment of how they may or may not function in that particular country's social, cultural, political and economic environment. This is particularly dangerous where highly concessional loans are involved, since SSE-DFIs may agree to ideas which they really find unacceptable in order to obtain the concessional terms.

Donors can nevertheless perform a valuable role by introducing new concepts and ideas, such as credit guarantee schemes, venture capital funds, factoring services and leasing, which help to strengthen the small enterprise sector. Donors can help to implement these ideas by providing advice, technical assistance, equity and loan funds. IFCT has, for instance, worked with the International Finance Corporation in setting up a leasing company, with the Commonwealth Development Corporation in forming a factory development company, and has used counterpart funds from Kreditanstalt fur Wiederaufbau (KfW) to invest in a small industry credit guarantee scheme.

CENTRAL DE CRÉDITO COOPERATIVO (CCC)

Mr. MARIO VALDEZ
Head SSE Department
CCC
Peru

INTRODUCTION

Central de Crédito Cooperativo del Peru (CCC) was established in 1961, without any government assistance, as a centralized cooperative agency to service the needs of some 75 cooperative savings and loans unions, spread throughout the country. Over the years the membership increased to over 300 unions, which led to rapid expansion. In its early days, CCC's attention was focused exclusively on its members.

In 1982 there was a major change in policies: CCC opened its doors to the general public and entered the financial market at large. From that time on, its major source of funding became public savings and deposits. Within the next two years CCC opened 17 branch offices and 37 agencies, not only in Lima where the headquarters are located, and other major cities, but in villages and remote areas throughout the country. CCC was particularly successful in attracting deposits in rural areas where there are few commercial banks. Deposits have over the last few years been growing at an average annual rate of over 200 per cent, although this figure must be read in the context of a turbulent economic situation with three-digit inflation.

The decision to start operating outside the cooperative sector appears to have ensured the institution's survival, in spite of Peru going through the worst economic crisis in its history. Numerous cooperatives were still lending and borrowing at traditionally low interest rates, while inflation reached levels of 125 per cent per annum and more. As a result a number of cooperatives have gone bankrupt, while others have been saved by being converted into CCC branch offices.

This has clearly demonstrated the need to operate at market rates of interest, whether the objectives are commercial or social. CCC was forced to compete directly with commercial banks and with savings and loans associations, especially in Lima itself. Financial services to private customers were developed and expanded, a vigorous advertising campaign was started and CCC paid some of the highest rates of interest in the financial marketplace. Services such as the five to one loans whereby individuals could borrow up to five times the amount they had saved, were particularly successful. Other financial instruments such as current accounts, funds transfers, commercial discounting and short-term loans were also introduced.

CCC's main strategies are to achieve real rather than merely nominal asset growth, to develop an integrated group of activities including credit insurance, social activities, education, debt collections and data processing without increasing staff, to move in the direction of becoming a full service commercial and development bank and to provide assistance to small-scale enterprises and marginal groups, including the agricultural sector.

By the end of 1984 CCC had over 300 employees and its total assets were worth over US$ 11.5 million.

SERVICES TO SMALL ENTERPRISES

The staff of CCC are well aware of the social differences within the population. In order to be able to communicate with small-scale entrepreneurs and informal sector enterprises, it is necessary to learn not to be paternalistic, to learn from them as well as to assist them, and to avoid theoretical notions which are copied from other countries and are locally inapplicable.

We have to accept that we must learn from and work with marginal individuals and groups in order to assist them. This may be the last chance, given the economic crisis in Peru, to demonstrate the role of a development finance institution. The programme with credit cooperatives, and with small enterprises, is a living example of the kind of change that must be introduced in a country in which a large proportion of poor people's children do not reach the age of five.

In 1984 CCC signed a loan agreement with FMO. This is a good example of how foreign assistance can be genuinely valuable: both sides participated in the planning, project development, assistance and supervision. Peru's culture and conditions were duly considered, so that CCC's organization was substantially improved. Experience with other foreign agencies has not been the same.

The savings and loan cooperatives generally made loans for purchases such as household appliances, vehicles or school fees; very little credit was used for productive activities, apart from a certain amount of working capital for shop keepers and small traders. CCC is now focusing more attention on providing credit to productive enterprises through the Productive Credit Programme (PCP). Through this programme, a number of services are made available to small enterprises.

Studies indicate that only 12 per cent of Peruvian entrepreneurs have had any technical training, 25 per cent have had no secondary education and 16 per cent did not even finish primary school. Only 15 per cent have had any technical assistance, and less than 20 per cent have received any institutional credit. Almost half have no bank accounts, and the minority who have had bank loans have only borrowed for working capital purposes, and have covered less than two thirds of their requirements for this type of finance.

CCC has thus concluded that credit cannot be provided in isolation; it must be one part of a package which includes technical assistance, training and other forms of help, if we are to achieve our objectives of increasing employment, raising income levels and enhancing productivity. We prefer to concentrate on working capital loans, since there is already a great deal of underused plant in small enterprises in Peru. Government banks insist on a package which includes fixed and working capital, because this is demanded by certain foreign lenders, and CCC attempts to satisfy the unfulfilled demand for working capital.

Finance is provided on a tailor-made basis for each client, with conditions such as the term and grace period based on the application. CCC prefers, when possible, to provide working capital on the basis of a renewable line of credit with an average three-month term, taking the purpose of the request into account. Fixed asset loans are separately scheduled and then consolidated according to cash flow. Our experience with entrepreneurs shows that credit and collections can provide a valuable development experience, as well as satisfying financial needs.

TRAINING AND OTHER NON-FINANCIAL SERVICES

Credit applicants can generally be classified into two groups: some are existing clients or new ones who have clear objectives and experience, while others are very vague, generally having no more than a creative idea.

CCC endeavours to follow up credit with individual visits and to provide a degree of supervision, difficult though this is, but the emphasis will depend on the experience and the size of the enterprise. Training is provided by SENATI, the national industrial training organization, under a contract with CCC.

Typical training courses provide components on self-diagnosis, costing, production, marketing and market-surveys, credit sources and cash flow. There is an annual programme of courses, covering Lima and the provinces, but although CCC had some influence on the course design, the training did not achieve the desired result because of inadequate training methods and the limited experience of the instructors.

CCC now intends to provide three levels of technical assistance: in addition to the courses run by SENATI, an industrial engineer and other technical consultants have been contracted to provide individual assistance and CCC's own employees, working through the loan analyst, also assist in training and advice.

Experience with training methods applied by some public institutions suggests that participants are not sufficiently interested and their practical questions go unanswered. The courses are academically designed, and it is preferable to include group dynamics and group studies, case studies which relate to the reality of technical and management problems actually experienced by entrepreneurs, and problems which are drawn from CCC's experience with local small enterprises.

The entrepreneurs should pay something, even if it is only a symbolic payment, for individual technical assistance and training. Government technical assistance is sometimes unsound because the project evaluation is based on formal guarantees and details such as financial ratios rather than the complete picture including marketing, production, finance and the practical problems of the entrepreneurs. In addition, the technical advisers cannot maintain contact with entrepreneurs because of frequent changes in their organization.

It is also important that entrepreneurs should be guided through the channels whereby they can obtain assistance. Such guidance is necessary in the area of quality control and industrial standards, sub-contracting, export assistance and industrial estates. Credit should not be approached as an island; CCC's policy is to provide a complete set of services including training, consultancy and supervised credit in order to improve entrepreneurs' administration and productivity, to make them aware of their problems and personal deficiencies, to identify the bottle-necks in their organizations and to make genuine improvements. It is said to be important that CCC's training and technical assistance methods should relate effectively to the particular problems experienced by cooperatives and individual enterprises. Whenever possible, training and assistance are provided on the basis of a contract between the entrepreneur and CCC, working towards specific goals which are agreed by both sides.

THE INFORMAL SECTOR

The informal sector is a special case. It has been estimated that in this period of economic crisis some 70 per cent of the labour force of Lima is in the informal sector. An even higher proportion of some types of services, such as furniture manufacturing or transport, are provided by informal operators. Banks have recently recognized that they are unable to provide funds to the informal sector, because of their need to work at a profit and the regulations which effect their lending.

CCC must face this challenge, since there is a serious need. Informal operators in Lima have very little capital, they cannot provide traditional guarantees such as fixed assets because they use second-hand equipment, or none at all, and they have no information or training on financial administration. The individual operators have to come together in order to avail themselves of credit, technical assistance and training. Reciprocal approaches, such as solidarity groups, have to be tried out as an alternative tool to make people aware of their responsibility to avoid negligence. CCC has recently signed a contract with the Pan American Union in order to facilitate services of this kind.

CCC feels that it must enter this sector, because official regulations prevent the commercial banks from providing

assistance to informal entrepreneurs, and because the loans are
expensive to administer and do not provide good margins. CCC
plans to provide loans to informal operators on behalf of other
organizations who provide guarantees. The Pan American Union
has deposited a dollar fund with CCC to guarantee loans to the
informal sector and provide an indirect source of finance, and
CCC is also working with CARE in this field.

Larger and more organized small enterprises may require
other services such as discounting, letters of credit and so on
and CCC must adapt its services to the differing needs of its
clients. It is important, however, to avoid using loans to
formalize informal operators. The costs of formalization, such
as tax administration and legal problems, mean that
formalization at an early stage renders the smallest
enterprises uneconomic.

Small loans are costly and it may be difficult to achieve
the desired volume which is necessary for viability. Medium-
scale loans can provide some element of cross-subsidy, and can
also give tangible evidence of employment development through
finance.

Every case must be dealt with on its merits; some
enterprises require marketing and export advice, or
introductions and special financial assistance for social
projects. In one case, for instance, a group of women in a
poor fishing village has been assisted by CCC in exporting its
handicraft products. As has been stated before, it is
important to avoid a pre-packaged approach; every client must
be treated on his or her own merits.

PROBLEMS OF INSTITUTIONALIZATION

The severe economic crisis which has affected Peru since 1982
has made it very difficult to institutionalize this programme.
The continuing devaluation and inflation of the currency has
had a considerable impact both on the cost of money and on the
enterprises themselves.

It has been necessary to charge a high effective rate of
interest in order to cover the exchange losses on the FMO loan.
Small enterprises borrow in local currency but the loan must be
repaid in foreign currency, and the rate of devaluation has
exceeded that of inflation. In an attempt to cover this risk,
CCC has set up a foreign exchange risk fund; up to 40 per cent
of the foreign exchange funds provided by FMO, together with 50
per cent of CCC's surplus, has been paid into this fund. This
may not be enough, but through harsh operating economies CCC
has so far managed to survive.

The economic recession has caused further problems. The
value of salaries has gone down, thus reducing internal demand,
and protectionism among industrialized countries has reduced
the demand for exports. As a result, industrial borrowers have
suffered from lower sales and have thus been unable to avail
themselves of credit opportunities.

In such conditions, loan applications must be carefully scrutinized in order to avoid overtrading, excess financial risks and subsequent negligence. The banks have generally responded to this problem by reducing their loan portfolio and increasing their investments in dollar certificates and other foreign assets. The effects of this have been clearly shown in the level of bad debts, which increased on some banks from six per cent to almost twenty per cent of their total loan portfolio. This generally requires special provisions and had consequent effects on the financial results.

Further problems arose from the variation in rates of interest which could be charged because of government policies. The following table demonstrates the instability and rapid changes in interest rates which were dictated by government policies and the economic situation.

December	1984	154% effective rate	
February	1985	190%	'' ''
July	1985	273%	'' ''
4 August	1985	110%	'' ''
26 August	1985	72%	'' ''
October	1985	50%	'' ''

As can be seen, the government is making determined steps to reduce the rate of inflation, and as from August 1985 the maximum effective rate of interest which can be charged has been significantly reduced. If the government does not succeed in reducing inflation, however, it will be impossible to charge positive real interest rates and the effect on the real value of CCC's portfolio will be serious. In addition, pressure arises from CCC's traditional customers, since cooperative unions expect to pay something lower than the prevailing rate of interest.

Small enterprises, on the other hand, appear not to be unduly affected by interest rate changes. In the informal sector, borrowing on a daily basis, annual rates of 800 to 1000 per cent are not uncommon; on the other hand, the losses on loans to cooperative unions are negligible, whereas it is too early to say what CCC'S loan experience with small enterprise clients will be. The rapid changes in interest rates cause further problems in that the demand for loans is reduced, since prospective borrowers find it very difficult to plan ahead.

There have also been problems in the internal organization. Initially, a decentralized pattern was selected, whereby separate departments were set up for lending, operations, collections and so on. Technical assistance was provided by SENATI, under contract to CCC, and although this did not involve CCC's own employees there had to be a substantial degree of coordination between the loan officers and SENATI staff.

Experience has revealed that this is not an adequate structure. There has been insufficient coordination,

43

particularly when inflation and heavy competition required maximum efficiency. It has also been impossible for the loan division to devote sufficient time to the new programme, because of its other activities.

It was thus decided, in August 1985, to centralize the small enterprise lending in a specialised unit, though this has not yet been completely implemented. It was also decided to improve the quality of technical assistance which has not been sufficiently high because of the lack of experience and inappropriate methods used by the government agencies. In addition technical follow-up was inadequate. It is therefore planned to contract individual experts on an hourly basis to provide the necessary services.

FUTURE PROSPECTS

In addition to its own organization, and to providing better training and technical services to medium and small-scale borrowers, CCC has a number of other prospects for the future. In addition to working towards the general goal of conversion into a commercial and development bank, plans are being worked on in order to cooperate with other institutions to provide finance to groups of informal sector operators. The government has also decreed that there should be certain special 'micro regions' in the more depressed areas of the country, and CCC hopes to provide special assistance in these areas, in collaboration with other agencies.

CCC also intends to provide more credit to agricultural and food-related industries. In 1950, 61 per cent of Peru's population lived in rural areas but by 1980 this had decreased to 40 per cent. The number of people employed in agriculture decreased by 7 per cent over this time, but this was not the result of higher productivity. More credit and development is required in the rural areas if food production is to be increased.

Finally, CCC is anxious to assist its clients to take advantage of foreign marketing opportunities, in an effort to compensate for the reduced local demand caused by the economic crisis. It is to be hoped, in summary, that CCC, in collaboration with other institutions, can make a significant contribution to resolving Peru's problems through providing an integrated package of assistance to medium, small and informal sector entrepreneurs.

PLANTERS DEVELOPMENT BANK (PDB)

Mr. J. TAMBUNTING
President
Planters Development Bank
The Philippines

INTRODUCTION

The experience of Planters Development Bank (PDB) shows that it is possible for a privately owned institution to be engaged mainly in financing the requirements of small enterprises, in spite of the additional social costs involved, while retaining its commercial viability. PDB is somewhat different from most development financing institutions, and it may therefore be useful to examine the nature of the bank's current operations, and the process by which the bank attained its current position.

Unlike most other SSE-DFI's, Planters Development Bank has a full range of domestic commercial banking facilities. It has access to domestic funds through savings, fixed term and demand deposits, it provides domestic trade credits and is also involved in housing finance. In one sense Planters Development Bank may be classified as a Hybrid SSE-DFI.

Planters Development Bank was transformed from what might be called a pure development finance institution to a hybrid because of the need to overcome certain factors which might otherwise have inhibited its growth. The bank started out as a pure development institution, heavily dependent on government subsidy. Its initial activities were confined to term financing and a government re-discounting scheme which allowed PDB's meagre funds to be replaced. Because PDB's resources were limited, because its offices were located throughout the countryside and because there were no private institutions apparently serving small enterprises it was very easy to determine that Planters Development Bank's natural market was those entrepreneurs whose financial needs were relatively small and who were generally located outside the Metro Manila area.

When the present owners took over PDB in 1972, they realized that government subsidies and other support were not permanent. Because of other national priorities, they accepted that government assistance would eventually be removed; the only thing that was unclear was when this would take place. In anticipation of these changes, management drew up plans to enable PDB to remain viable on a purely commercial basis. Planters Development Bank continues to seek out and obtain concessional financing when this is available, but does not rely on it.

At the end of 1984, Planters Development Bank's outstanding loan portfolio amounted to some US$ 13 million, representing around 62 per cent of PDB's total resources. Over 40 per cent of this amount was for financing food production and manufacturing activities, while the balance was lent for real estate, public utilities and the services sector.

Two thousand, three hundred and forty-three loans, or 87 per cent of the total, were lent to small-scale businesses, and they constituted 61 per cent of the total amount of money. Small enterprise loans range from a minimum of US$ 6,500 to US$ 80,000; Planters Development Bank has so far made very few start-up loans, but plans are in hand to deal with this field in the future.

Over 85 per cent of PDB's loans was to enterprises outside Metro Manila. Because of PDB's familiarity with rural areas, and its branch network, it has been feasible to increase lending to agricultural projects. Loans for agriculture, and in particular the pilot programme for very small farm loans, will be implemented gradually since this is a risky and less profitable field.

Thirty-nine per cent of the money lent is on a short-term basis, with a maturity of one year or less; small enterprise loan maturities are determined on the basis of debt-servicing capacity, not on the life of the assets which have been purchased, since it is felt that there is some risk that surplus funds might be diverted to non-productive investments if they did not have to be repaid.

Prior to the current economic crisis in the Philippines, the arrears rate on small enterprise loans was running at around seven per cent; it has now increased, it is hoped temporarily, to between 17 and 18 per cent. The interest rate varies in accordance with the cost of funds, particularly in the present highly volatile economic circumstances, but it is PDB's policy to aim at a spread of between seven and ten per cent. There has, so far, been sufficient demand from applicants with collateral for PDB not to have to accept unsecured loans. Discussions are, nevertheless, being undertaken with FMO in order to enable PDB to lend on an unsecured basis.

DIVERSIFICATION OF FUND SOURCES

Planters Development Bank has always attempted to be active and innovative in seeking out a diversified funding base in order to reduce its reliance on government support and to avoid being stifled by a lack of resources. For this reason, PDB has placed great emphasis on generating public deposits and on setting up a network of offices in order to widen its market and make its deposit and lending facilities accessible to as many clients as possible.

PDB has expanded its branch network slowly, opening only a few offices at a time, because it takes a while for branches to attain viability and PDB cannot afford a substantial drain on its resources. PDB has also tried to keep its operating cost down by having the minimum number of staff at each branch and keeping its operations as simple as possible. As a result, during the 1970s, branches were able to break even with a deposit base of only US$ 100,000, and it was possible to obtain this level within the first year of their operation.

Because PDB relies on deposits to fund its medium and long-term lending, there is a problem of properly matching maturities of fund sources and uses. Experience suggests that the stable portion of PDB's deposits comprises around 85 per cent of the total amount, compelling PDB to set aside at least 15 per cent of its deposit liabilities in highly liquid form. The bank is also required by law to maintain its deposit liabilities in very low-yielding assets, which effectively increases the cost of funds. Because of this and because of the volatile portion of its deposits, PDB's lending rates are higher than those charged by bigger institutions. It has, however, been possible to counteract this disadvantage by better delivery and service quality, and this trade-off is widely accepted by small enterprise borrowers.

PDB has always searched for new sources of inexpensive funds, on a short and long-term basis, as well as developing its deposit base. Whenever a new government-funded or sponsored financing programme has been announced, the bank has always been the first to apply for accreditation and to make use of the funding for lending through the extensive branch network. Funds which have been used on this basis include the World Bank Rural Credit Programme, the Industrial Guarantee and Loan Fund, the World Bank Small and Medium Industry Programme, the Quedan Guarantee Fund and the Guarantee Fund for Small and Medium Enterprises. In the process, PDB has been able to provide relatively inexpensive long-term funds to small enterprise borrowers while achieving a perfectly matched maturity between its sources and applications of funds.

PDB has also established credit lines with other financial institutions. Although these are of short maturity, they help to ensure that funds are readily available and that loans can thus be disbursed to clients as they are required. They also allow the bank to take advantage of low rates whenever the money market allows this.

COPING WITH THE RISKS IN SSE FINANCING

In order to deal with the constraints inherent in financing small enterprises, Planters Development Bank has gradually built its institutional capability within the limits of its own modest resources. Because it is fairly small, PDB has not been able to organize full-scale units to discharge some of the essential functions, and has in the process been forced to improvise or to employ apparently second best solutions which have nevertheless proved to be just as effective.

Because of the small average loan size, the administration costs of small enterprise financing are well-known to be very high. In order to minimize the impact of these high costs, the bank has adopted a portfolio mix and, rather than lending only to small enterprises, has decided to continue lending to those clients who have grown to become medium-scale enterprises. In addition, part of the portfolio has been devoted to the short-term financing needs of clients, thus allowing a faster turn-over and simpler and less expensive evaluation process. Short-term and medium-scale loans thus indirectly subsidize the long-term and small enterprise portfolio, and the Bank has been able to offset the high administration cost incurred by its small enterprise accounts in this way.

The costs of appraising small enterprise loan applications also tend to be high because the entrepreneurs lack book-keeping and financial management skills. More often than not, PDB has to reconstruct their records and to prepare financial projections for them. PDB has accepted these costs and has also added to them because its staff are expected to be involved in preparing applicants' feasibility studies. PDB believes that by doing this, it has become more familiar with projects and has thus been able to cut down later supervision or default costs by screening out potentially bad loans from the beginning.

Because PDB cannot possibly afford full-scale supervision departments to cover all the areas it serves, it has been decided to lay more stress on effective product identification and appraisal. In addition to training its lending staff in these fields, the bank attempts to be as familiar as possible with the industries it serves, and, through its branches, to establish intimate and continuing relationships with its clients. Managers of local origin are preferred, and are recruited for their marketing ability as well as for their potential as lending officers and extension workers.

It is well-known that small enterprise borrowers tend to use the proceeds of loans for non-productive purposes, particularly if loans are made at concessional rates of interest. It is also difficult to monitor businesses because basic accounting systems are absent. For this reason, most small enterprise borrowers have to be closely supervised.

Planters Development Bank, however, because it cannot afford to maintain full supervision services, has adopted a system of 'supervision by exception'. Borrowers are asked, as a basic requirement, to set up and maintain an acceptable accounting system, and the bank is willing to assist with this, either directly or through consultants. Loan disbursements have to be made direct to suppliers and the borrowers are required to submit evidence of purchases. Apart from this and annual visits to businesses and periodic reviews of financial statements, there is no regular follow-up on borrowers who pay on time, and there is no supervision unless payments run into arrears. Fortunately, because the law requires that its loans are secured, PDB's clients are more or less guaranteed to maintain reasonable financial discipline.

NON-FINANCIAL SERVICES

In order to strengthen its small enterprise client's operations, Planters Development Bank provides a variety of non-financial support, largely on an informal basis, in order to minimize its cost. These services include management counselling, which is provided to correct the weaknesses that may have been revealed during the appraisal and implementation process. If the entrepreneur or his staff lack the necessary skills, PDB recommends outside consultants to perform whatever functions have not been effectively carried out. PDB's lending officers help loan applicants to install accounting systems and refer them to professional accountants to assist in this work. The bank staff also assist in the preparation of feasibility studies, in order to gain familiarity with the operation, and are encouraged to suggest changes to proposals in order to ensure that they are as economical and profitable as possible.

PDB's own staff, or, where necessary, outside consultants, help entrepreneurs to analyze their operations, and recommend improvements. Entrepreneurs are also helped to identify possible partners for joint-ventures, and are introduced to prospective buyers who may be known to the bank. If clients need additional financing, either in the form of loans or equity, the bank is able to introduce them to other sources of funds, and, through its affiliate companies, Planters Development Bank extends insurance, technical and other managerial services to its clients.

DIVERSIFICATION OF INCOME SOURCES

In order to off-set the high cost of small enterprise lending and to ensure its continued viability, PDB has attempted to diversify its income by entering certain other related activities, albeit cautiously. Housing mortgages have been offered under the national shelter programme, and this risk-free activity, as well as providing a sizeable source of income, has enabled the bank to develop lasting relationships with clients of high income potential.

PDB has also invested in the share capital of some corporations who are working in allied areas. As a complement to its mortgage activities, PDB has invested in a real estate company, so that it can on its own account obtain prime real estate property and make profits through residential construction. Planters Development Bank has also established an insurance agency, which both contributes to the bank's income and provides insurance advice and services to its clients. An investment has also been made in an investment and management company for serving small enterprises, which has led the bank, indirectly, into equity investments and specialized technical and managerial assistance to its clients.

In the context of straightforward banking activities, Planters Development Bank provides domestic letters of credit and current accounts, and during the past three years, the bank has earned a total of over $1.5 million from these additional sources of revenue, representing some 15 per cent of PDB's total revenue during the period. This has provided the bank with an important cushion to absorb some of the higher initial costs attributable to lending to small enterprise.

As has already been indicated, however, these additional services have allowed the bank to offer a 'one stop' service to its clients, enabling them to obtain an optimum package of services and enabling the bank to become more familiar with its client's operations. PDB's branch managers have come to be regarded as financial advisers and not merely bankers, and have thus been able to maintain an open and cooperative relationship with their clients. Equally important, borrowers have been given credit for the earnings which have been derived from the other facilities they use, and the interest rate they pay has been able to be reduced.

FUTURE PROSPECTS

In the future, Planters Development Bank believes that there are tremendous opportunities in small enterprise lending, because of the current Philippine government policy and the fact that more and more funds are being made available for re-lending to this sector. The bank intends to continue its deep involvement in small enterprise lending, and because of the many untapped opportunities and the potential of their impact on national development, the bank is bound to increase its participation in this sector. If it were wholly dependent on its own resources, however, PDB would take longer than desirable to make a genuinely significant impact.

For a number of reasons, the risks in small enterprise lending are normally considered to be greater than those in lending to larger businesses. Private institutions, such as Planters Development Bank, with significant financial responsibility to the public, are substantially limited in their ability to take risks. It may therefore be necessary to create an institution to absorb some of these inherent credit risks, in order to encourage and stimulate a greater flow of credit resources to small business.

It is likewise important to strengthen the bank's own funding base. If PDB's risk lending continues to be expanded, its equity must be increased to conform to statutory limitations. There may, however, be insufficient domestic resources for this purpose, and it has therefore been necessary to look beyond the Philippines for equity investments. The FMO owns 18 per cent of Planters Development Bank, and has thus made a significant contribution to the development and strengthening of a concrete example of a 'hybrid' SSE-DFI which has been able, with some degree of success, to reconcile development objectives with commercially oriented banking activities.

USAID AND SSE-DFIs

Mr. L. READE
Deputy Assistant Administrator
Bureau for Private Enterprise
Agency for International Development
U.S.A

INTRODUCTION

The Agency for International Development (AID) has had extensive experience in wholesaling credit through financial intermediaries in developing countries. Beginning in the 1960s, AID was instrumental in strengthening those institutions in Latin America known as Financieras and in creating the savings and loan system focused on the financing of housing and related infrastrucure in Latin America and the Caribbean. Since that time, AID has helped to create and support literally dozens of development finance institutions around the world.

AID has also financed programmes for on-lending to farmers, farm-related industry, rural enterprises and urban industrial sector enterprises, including very small businesses or micro-enterprises. The intermediaries have been governments, central banks, ministries, public sector financial institutions, regional development banks, and, increasingly, private sector development finance institutions and the banking system as a whole, through rediscounting operations. More recently, other private intermediaries, many of a type new to AID's portfolio, have been enlisted as credit vehicles.

The reason for using wholesale intermediaries for the distribution of credit is clear: staff constraints and administrative costs make it impractical for donor agencies to make very small loans. Direct lending is only efficient when it is to governments or to larger private corporations.

In general, AID's experience suggest that, to be successful, development finance institutions should rely on private sector markets to determine the mix and the allocation of their resources. This conclusion is not a matter of ideology or doctrine, it is the result of trial and error over a period of years. The optimum mix of resources should therefore consist of unsubsidized equity and debt funds, and those funds should be on-lent to small enterprises at unsubsidized market rates of interest.

It is also important to pay explicit attention to the effect of the mix of resources on the long-term financial viability of the institution. Due attention must be paid to foreign exchange risks, liquidity and the maintenance of capital values.

AID AND ITS FOCUS ON THE PRIVATE SECTOR

AID's programmes attempt to reach the poor majority, that is the people who are lower than the average in terms of income in a given area. One way of reaching this target group is through assisting small and medium size private enterprises. Such enterprises have to prove themselves in the marketplace without the benefit of special government favours or collusive market power. They are forced to be innovative and efficient, they tend to be less capital-intensive than large firms and to have more of an impact on creating jobs. Their employees, for the most part, come from the poor majority.

In recognition of this vital role of private enterprise as an engine of development, AID established the Bureau for Private Enterprise (BPE) in 1981 to drive a programme throughout the agency, emphasizing the use of market forces.

The Private Sector Revolving Fund, a self-replenishing mechanism through which Bureau loans are channelled principally to development finance institutions, was established by Congress in November 1983. This marked a significant change in emphasis that has affected the substance of much of AID's financing.

The following figures illustrate the impact of this policy. In the four years ending 31 August 1984, AID financed 196 private sector projects, totalling a little over US$ 1.2 billion, that is a rate of US$ 300 million per annum. If 75 multi-sectoral loans, and 12 loans which were basically for balance of payment purposes are excluded, 31 financial loans amounting to over US$ 316 million were by far the largest part. Loans to development finance institutions constituted 40 per cent of the total portfolio, and the second largest part, 24 per cent, was for agricultural purposes, much of which was also handled through wholesaling intermediaries.

AID's policy is fundamentally the same for small and large-scale enterprises, except that the vital role of technical assistance is duly recognized, through monetary assistance which may reach as much as ten per cent of the amount lent. Lending to SSE-DFIs is not trouble free; the main challenges which continue to be confronted by AID are interest-rate policy and conditionality, the strengthening of institutions, and how to reach the target group, particularly the informal sector, more effectively.

INTEREST-RATE POLICY

AID believes that loans to development finance institutions should be made at or near market rates of interest wherever possible, and that loans by such institutions should always be at full market rates. What is the reason for this insistence? It has been learned through trial and error that subsidized interest rates tend to subvert development. This is because they allocate funds to those borrowers that need them least,

52

they promote the over-use of capital-intensive technologies that create little employment and they discriminate against private sector borrowers in favour of the public sector.

Interest rates are a market mechanism whereby limited funds are allocated among those who are willing and able to pay for them. As with any commodity, if the price is unreasonably low, the available supply will not be sufficient to accommodate all potential buyers, thereby creating shortages of funds. In the case of loans, what are the effects of such shortages?

Studies validate what logic dictates: in these circumstances, lenders lend to those who least need the money. The biggest and least risky clients receive the loans and the small and medium-sized enterprises go without. In order to minimize the risks, the lenders exact physical collateral guarantees which small enterprises cannot provide. The self-defeating consequence of subsidized interest rates is that the borrower whom the government is trying to help is excluded and, in fact, ends up paying far higher rates in informal credit markets. This conclusion is confirmed by studies which show without question that for small enterprises, it is not the cost of capital but access to capital which is crucial to their viability and growth.

Subsidized interest rates also make it more difficult for finance institutions to maintain the real spreads between the cost of funds and the rates charged which are necessary to avoid erosion of capital. With 25 per cent inflation, for instance, a development finance institution would have to charge a 6.25 per cent spread in order to maintain a five per cent spread in real terms to cover the costs of operation. If the institution charges a nominal five per cent spread, it will obtain only four per cent in real terms and decapitalization will inevitably occur unless the institution can cut its cost. The result, in AID's experience, is that institutions restrict their lending to their larger and less risky clients, effectively encluding small enterprises from the market. In particular, entrepreneurs who are starting businesses for the first time, and who thus constitute the highest risk, are the least likely to be funded. SSE-DFIs should be free to charge them somewhat higher rates, to allow for the higher risks involved.

Another perverse effect of underpricing capital through subsidized interest rates is that it promotes its over-use by those who are fortunate enough to obtain the loans. Borrowers rationally choose technologies which use more capital and less labour than they would otherwise have chosen, had the interest rates been higher. For the country as a whole, the more capital used, the greater the foreign debt incurred and the less employment generated. This is a counter-productive economic strategy for a developing country to pursue.

Finally, subsidized interest rates constitute an irresistible lure for public sector enterprises. Governments often find it easier to pressure development finance institutions to lend to public sector enterprises, than to finance those enterprises wholly and directly from the central budget.

These considerations have led AID to seek positive real interest rates to ensure that the available funds will go to the most productive users. Since interest rate policy is determined by government and not by the marketplace alone, AID has put this subject high on the agenda for policy dialogue with host governments. AID makes its view clear, and tries, when necessary, to convince governments to adapt their policies.

STRENGTHENING THE INSTITUTIONS

A major objective of AID in its work with SSE-DFIs is to strengthen the institutions themselves as well as their clients. Typically, this objective is expressed by efforts to provide technical assistance in order to increase the institution's efficiency and its ability to analyse projects. This assistance is intended to decrease the costs for the SSE-DFIs, and their clients, and to improve management information systems, spreads and the analysis of profit centres.

Project analysis is also a principle of AID. There are two aspects to this, financial and economic analysis. Financial analysis should satisfy the lender that the investment will generate the cash flow necessary to service the loan. This means that collateral guarantees become less important.

The difference between financial and economic analysis poses a greater problem. This involves the possible differences between what is financially good for the borrowing firm, and the SSE-DFI, and what is good for the country and society as a whole. If markets are imperfect (as they always are), if unemployment and underemployment are problems (as they usually are), and if exchange rates overvalue the domestic currency (as they often do), then it is quite possible that a privately profitable undertaking can impoverish the country as a whole. Hence it is necessary to carry out economic and social as well as financial analysis. This poses the dilemma of who should do the socio-economic analysis, and how sophisticated it should be. This is not an easy decision.

Ideally, the government should do the analysis because it is the government's policy which has had the major influence in making it necessary. In most countries, however, AID's experience is that government involvement in analysis produces interminable delays and endless paperwork. It is preferable, therefore, that the development finance institutions should carry out the analysis themselves. This should, however, be a very simple and approximate analysis, which provides some safeguards against the sponsorship of clearly anti-social investments, rather than a fine-tuned and full-scale academic study of each proposal.

REACHING THE TARGET GROUP

AID's third major area of interest is the problem of how to reach the poor majority in developing countries. This addresses both humanitarian and development objectives: humanitarian because economic development should enrich human life, and development because progress largely springs from the innovative efforts of new entrepreneurs and smaller firms which are not part of the existing power establishment. How can SSE-DFIs, through their on-lending, reach this target group?

One step in this direction is to replace traditional banking criteria with project analysis as a means of judging credit-worthiness. The SSE-DFI has to decide whether it is more important that the proposed loan will be used for an investment which itself generates the income necessary to service it, or whether the collateral for the loan will cover the risk whether or not the business is a good one. The trade-off between analysis and risk requires, as noted above, that the SSE-DFI should add to its banking skills an ability to analyse projects beyond the traditional banking criteria of credit-worthiness. If the institution emphasizes project analysis rather than collateral, it is more likely to qualify small borrowers for the limited supply of loanable funds and thus to confer benefits on the target group.

The banking community as a whole could reach more members of the target group by jointly financing a credit guarantee insurance fund from the spread charged on loans to small enterprises. Such a fund permits the institution to hedge part of its risk on loans which are short of traditional collaterals. AID's experience with such funds is limited, and it is too early to reach final conclusions. The experience has been, however, that such funds are usually profitable. The introduction of better project analysis decreases the actual risk to a level which is below the perceived risk of the lender, and thus permits such a fund to generate a surplus.

Another important way in which development finance institutions can reach small businesses is to use positive real interest rates in the evaluation of proposals and allocation of funds. As has already been mentioned, the availability rather than the price of formal credit is the main problem for small enterprises. The alternative, especially for very small businesses in the informal sector, is to seek credit from loan sharks. These people provide a valuable service. They do lend money, and they lend quickly, albeit at very high rates of interest. Development finance institutions should compete with them, and not eliminate them. Such competition will lower the cost of credit in the informal market and will also allow the institution to recognize the higher real cost of lending to small enterprises.

THE OPTIMUM MIX OF RESOURCES

The views of AID on interest-rates, strengthening institutions and lending to small enterprises provide a basis for discussing what mix of financial resources is most likely to enhance the long-term viability of a development finance institution. This question can be divided into two broad issues, one being that of external loans and foreign exchange risks, and the other the liquidity and maintenance of capital values.

External loans can be an important complement to the domestic resources of a DFI. They can and should be used to increase the level of domestic resources which can be obtained. There is a very real danger, however, of becoming too dependent on external resources. The problem, which is presently evident in much of Latin America and the Caribbean, is that external loans can compound a country's debt service problems if the resources are not properly used. As a general rule, external resources should only be used to finance domestic expenditures which add to domestically consumed output if the investments will also generate very high foreign exchange earnings or efficiently replace foreign exchange expenditures with domestic production. This will minimize the risk of overall foreign exchange losses, but the burden on the DFI, and its clients, may be unacceptable.

In 1984 the Bureau for Private Enterprise developed the concept of a 'Collateral Account' to minimize the foreign exchange risk involved in lending for domestic expenditure. The AID dollar loan is used to establish a standby letter of credit facility. This facility guarantees domestic lines of credit which are extended by local banks in local currency, rather than in foreign exchange, to small and medium-sized enterprises.

For example, such a structure has recently been used in a project with two 'financieras' in Latin America, to guarantee local currency borrowing. One serious constraint on the ability of the 'financieras' to make long-term loans is that they are unable to borrow on a long-term basis themselves. The beneficiaries of the letter of credit are the purchasers of development bonds issued by the 'financieras'. In this instance, the external loan from AID is intended to create a market for domestic savings which would otherwise not be made available. So long as the projects financed are sound, and the loans to small enterprises are serviced on schedule in domestic currency, the foreign exchange risk is eliminated.

In so far as loans are actually used for foreign exchange expenditure, however, foreign exchange risks are unavoidable; in this case, should the enterprise, the SSE-DFI or the government bear the foreign exchange losses which may occur? Many economists would argue that the ultimate borrower should bear the foreign exchange risk because depreciation in the value of local currency versus an external standard is usually accompanied by domestic inflation, which will allow the producer to raise prices. This case, however, is by no means clear. Foreign exchange losses usually result from government actions and macro-economic policy decisions, and the borrowers are often also faced with price controls.

Such factors are beyond the control of the lending institution and its clients, and consideration should be given to making the government responsible for them. In practice, however, this is often not feasible and the lending institution and its clients must bear the foreign exchange risks. It is therefore imperative that SSE-DFIs should seek ways to minimize their own and their clients' exposure to foreign exchange risks.

In an expanding economy, especially one which is suffering from high and erratic inflation, development finance institutions are threatened with liquidity problems and the erosion of their capital base. The use of short-term resources for longer-term lending is one source of problems. External loans, which are on longer-term basis, can mitigate liquidity threats to some extent.

The upper limits for debt equity ratios depend on circumstances which are specific to particular countries and institutions. If prudent limits are exceeded, however, the institution may be burdened with debt-servicing obligations which at times threaten its liquidity.

Many governments use portfolio and reserve requirements to influence the type and amount of lending. It is more difficult for development finance institutions to accommodate more rigorous requirements of this sort than it is for commercial banks, because their loans turn over less rapidly. This is often a source of major liquidity problems for development finance institutions. Similarly, changes in tax laws can have a greater negative impact on these institutions than on commercial banks, because of the differences in their lending periods.

The principal causes, however, of liquidity problems and decapitalization are inflation and negative real interest rates; for this reason, in addition to championing positive real interest rates, AID favours the use of variable interest loans made by development finance institutions. The alternative is for the institutions to charge higher-than-necessary constant nominal rates which include a premium to guard against the uncertainties of liquidity and decapitalization.

CONCLUSION

In summary, AID believes that market forces and private initiatives are most often the engines of development, and that the optimum mix of resources for development finance institutions must derive from this. AID policy dialogue with governments, and technical assistance to development finance institutions and their clients, should promote the efficiency of their lending to small enterprises.

AID continues to experiment with ways to reach the smaller entrepreneurs, to make informal sector enterprises eligible for formal credit and, through guarantee funds, rediscounting operations and collateral accounts, to decrease the risk, and the perception of risk, of development finance institutions in their lending operations to small enterprises.

KREDITANSTALT FÜR WIEDERAUFBAU (KfW) AND FINANCE FOR SMALL ENTERPRISE

Dr. H.R. HUCHTING-RADEKE, presented by Mr. W. ABEL
Kreditanstalt fur Wiederaufbau (KfW)
Frankfurt
Germany

INTRODUCTION

The Kreditanstalt fur Wiederaufbau (KfW) functions as a development bank both for the German economy and developing countries. In the latter capacity, KfW is responsible for funds which are channelled to developing countries under the official aid programme of the Federal Republic of Germany. KfW appraises the projects for all such financial transactions, on the basis of an agreement between KfW and the German Federal Government.

Assistance is provided to small enterprises through three different types of programmes: substantial funds have been channelled to small and medium enterprises through development banks; the subsidiary programme channels funds through German small and medium enterprises for investment in developing countries; and a special programme supports German Enterprises which intend to introduce new technologies in their subsidiary and technology programmes; by the end of 1984 some US$ 55 million and US$ 22 million respectively had been committed under these two programmes; this compares with a total of about US$ 1,300 million which has been committed, admittedly over a far longer period, through development banks. Some 83 per cent of this latter sum has been used to promote small and medium-sized enterprises.

Some 10 per cent of all official German technical cooperation funds to developing countries has been channelled through development banks, and about 83 per cent of this amount has been for the promotion of small and medium industry, with the balance of 17 per cent being for agricultural purposes. Sixty per cent of this total has been borrowed by banks in Asia, 14 per cent each in Latin America and Africa, and the balance in European banks from Portugal, Cyprus, Greece, Turkey and Israel.

To date, loans have been made to about 100 development banks in 51 different countries. Between 1979 and 1983 it has been estimated that these loans created about 160,000 jobs; the investment costs per job ranged generally between US$ 6000 and US$ 15,000.

Development banks play a particularly important role because they complement, functionally and regionally, the commercial banks in their countries and the informal credit sector, which plays a very important role in developing countries. KfW has only worked with commercial banks in a very limited number of countries. This is partly due to the fact that KfW's programmes are essentially on an inter-governmental basis, and developing country governments appear to favour their own rather than private commercial banks when this is possible.

Development banks provide access to institutional credit primarily for those parts of the population which do not obtain finance from commercial banks, for want of security or other reasons. Another important function of development banks is their promotion of the credit infrastructure, by mobilizing savings and introducing new types of clients to the banking sector.

In view of the target groups which they reach, it is clear why development banks are favoured as intermediaries for financial cooperation funds; in view of the relatively small amount involved in each sub-loan, and the need for monitoring large numbers of businesses, it is only possible to reach this target group with the help of local financing institutions.

Since lending to small enterprises involved a high workload, high costs and high risks, only a few development banks have specialized exclusively in this field. Most of the institutions supported by KfW make less than 30 per cent of their loans to small businesses.

Individual development banks differ greatly in their performance. A number of banks in sub-Saharan Africa, particularly, suffer from severe management weaknesses. This results in a lack of dynamism, inadequate project appraisals, insufficient monitoring and inadequate assistance to borrowers. Even if a great deal of consultancy assistance is provided, the working methods of these banks tend only to improve after very extended assignments. These problems are also, of course, the result of the difficult general economic situation, inadequate infrastructure and the shortage of entrepreneurial potential in many African countries. Because of these difficulties, these banks incur excessively high administration costs in relation to the amount of funds they borrow and on-lend.

THE SUBSIDIARY PROGRAMME

KfW makes low-cost loans to German small and medium enterprises, for investment in developing countries, under the subsidiary programme which was created in 1979. The German firms' sales should in principle not exceed 60 million US$ per annum, and the purpose of this programme is both to contribute to the economic development of the host country through private investment and to make it easier for German small and medium-sized enterprises to invest in developing countries.

Terms and conditions are favourable: projects in the least developed countries bear an interest rate of 2.5 per cent per annum, and those in other developing contries carry a 3.5 per cent interest rate. The total amount of the loan is disbursed. The loan may be given for a period of up to 15 years, including up to five years grace period. As a rule, 50 per cent of the costs of qualifying projects has to be borne by the German firm, and if the investment is of particular development significance KfW's share may even exceed that limit. The maximum amount per investment is in principle about US$ 700,000, but this can on occasion be exceeded.

KfW differentiates between investments financing and the financing of studies under this programme. Investment finance is designed to contribute to the costs of erection, expansion or acquisition of firms or of participation by the German firm in a joint-venture through equity or long-term lending. Studies of concrete well-defined projects, which have a reasonable chance of being implemented, can also be financed. Finance for such studies can only be made available to the German firm which intends to carry out the proposed project.

Between 1979 and the end of 1984 a total of some US$ 55 million was committed under the subsidiary programme for 290 investments in developing countries. The investments which have been made so far have required a total capital expenditure of nearly US$ 150 million, and have been intended to create some 21,000 new jobs in developing countries.

THE TECHNOLOGY PROGRAMME

The aim of the technology programme is to support small and medium-sized German firms which intend to introduce new technologies in factories in developing countries, within joint ventures with local partners. The scheme is designed to reduce the risks involved in technical innovations and to encourage the transfer of technology. The purpose of these loans is to bear a share of the total investment costs which will be borne by the German firms.

The terms and conditions of this scheme are very generous indeed. Interest is charged at a rate of one per cent for the period up to the beginning of repayment and 2.5 per cent thereafter. The loan term can be a maximum of fifteen years, including a grace period of up to five years. Security is not normally required. The loan generally amounts to up to 50 per cent of the investment to be made by the German firm, with a maximum of some US$ 700,000. If the borrower can prove that in the long run the new technology will not yield an adequate rate of return, KfW may partly or even fully waive repayment of interest, and even the loan itself.

If the information available is not sufficient for a decision to be made, a preparatory loan may be made to finance additional investigations, providing that the project has reasonable chance of being successfully implemented. Since the technology programme was started in 1981, 62 applications have been filed of which 42 have been approved.

PREREQUISITES FOR SUCCESSFUL SSE-DFIs

It can be concluded from KfW's experience with some 100 development banks involved in small enterprise lending, that there are a number of prerequisites which are likely to lead to successful operations. There should be a large network of branch offices, lending should be complemented with counselling, security requirements should be at least partially waived, and guarantee funds have an important role to play in this regard, lending procedures should be rapid and simple, there should be close contact with clients in order to make sure that the debt is serviced as agreed, and, in some cases, other agencies should be involved in related activities such as plant identification and selection, counselling and guarantees.

Numerous studies have proved that the demand for credit by small enterprises is independent of the interest rate charged by the formal sector; loans should therefore be made at market rates, and interest rates below market level should not be accepted. Market rates ensure an efficient allocation of capital in a macro-economic sense, they cover the high handling costs involved in small enterprise lending and prevent stronger and politically influential companies, which can borrow from other more appropriate sources and whose repayment behaviour, as has often been shown, is often worse than small borrowers, from being attracted to the funds which are intended for small enterprises.

Low-interest rates are particularly intolerable when they drop below the interest earned on savings deposits, thus leading to an artificial demand for credit and misdirection of capital. In addition negative real interest rates, which are below the prevailing rate of inflation, discourage the domestic saving which is necessary for the development of a credit infrastructure.

KfW generally requires development banks to charge interest rates which are at least in line with prevailing market rates. Any exceptions must be justified in detail by KfW in its appraisal report to the German Federal Ministry for Economic Cooperation. In most cases, such exceptions are justified by the development banks and KfW by reference to the particular needs of the target group. This of course contradicts the argument that small enterprise demand for credit is unaffected by interest rates, but the fact that such justification can be used demonstrates that KfW's influence on development banks' policies is limited.

KfW can use its influence to define the target group to which its credit should be on-lent, by confining its funds to certain regions, setting limits to the size of firms which are allowed to borrow or setting maximum investment costs per job. It is not possible, however, to steer the general business policies of development banks, by enforcing revised credit terms or in other ways. The same constraints also apply to the World Bank, so far as can be seen, although it lends far larger amounts of money to development banks than does KfW.

KFW'S SUPPORTING MEASURES FOR DEVELOPMENT BANKS

One way in which KfW supports SSE-DFIs is by paying for long or short-term consultancy assignments. Consultancy may also be provided to the ultimate borrowers, but this is less frequent. Such consultancy services are generally not financed from the loan itself but from additional resources which are given in a non-repayable grant. The consultancy is not directly tied to the KfW credit line, but is part of a general programme of assisting the development banks. It is financed and managed by the German Company for Technical Cooperation, or GTZ, which is in charge of assignments of this type. German finance for consultancy is especially needed when the development banks are newly established.

Another form of support is by granting higher spreads to development banks which use KfW loans for small-scale enterprise lending which involves a great deal of administrative work. The normal rule is to allow a spread of three per cent, but up to six per cent can be allowed in such cases.

Another instrument which is of some interest to development banks is an interest differential counterpart fund, which arises from the difference between the interest the development bank has to pay to KfW and the ultimate borrower's interest rate, less the agreed spread which can be used for special purposes to be agreed upon between KfW and the development bank. In this way, any margin over the six per cent maximum spread can be used to establish or assist a guarantee fund, to plan sectoral or regional investment programmes as a basis for project identification, for training, for increasing salaries of qualified staff in local branches, for support to training centres or vocational schools and other purposes.

Banks which have themselves to bear the foreign exchange risk, rather than it being borne by the state, naturally use the interest differential counterpart funds first and foremost for insuring themselves against this risk. One disadvantage of this instrument, however, is the fact that the funds are initially quite small, since they only build up as the development bank's lending activities get under way.

CONCLUSIONS

In general, KfW is in favour of small enterprise promotion through SSE-DFIs because of the important contribution small enterprises have to make for economic and social development. There is, moreover, no better way of channelling funds to small enterprises, and thus enabling them to create jobs at lower costs than large ones.

There are, however, a number of ways in which development banks are less efficient as channels for funds than they might be. Their administration is weak, leading to high losses and a shrinking capital base, the ultimate borrowers do not adhere to

repayment schedules, lending is not effectively coordinated
with consultancy and the bank gives insufficient attention to
its borrowers. Small enterprises are particularly important
clients because of their relatively low capital investment
needs, and their even lower need for foreign exchange. This
can however lead to problems, since financial cooperation funds
are mainly designed to finance fixed assets, and local currency
costs cannot normally be funded in this way. In addition, and
perhaps most importantly, the political situation in developing
countries is often very unfavourable for small and medium-scale
enterprises.

(NOTE: At the time of the seminar the exchange rate was
US$1 to DM 3.50. As the current dollar value vis à vis the DM
is much lower, the dollar values mentioned in this paper should
be read in this context.)

WORLD BANK LENDING FOR SMALL ENTERPRISE

Mr. J. LEVITSKY
Operations Advisor Industry Department
International Bank for Reconstruction and Development
U.S.A.

INTRODUCTION

Small enterprises have difficulty in obtaining access to loans from financing institutions for well-known reasons. These institutions believe that it is risky and administratively expensive to lend to small enterprises. They consider such loans to be unprofitable and accordingly limit their activity in this field. For this reason, both in industrialized and developing countries special publicly supported programmes have been initiated to help make more finance available to small enterprises. These programmes differ in detail but their aim is the same, to provide small enterprises with access to institutional finance for fixed assets and working capital at terms and conditions which are within the debt servicing capacity of the enterprise.

DEVELOPMENT FINANCE INSTITUTIONS

The earlier small enterprise lending programmes financed by the World Bank channelled funds through development finance institutions. Experience over the years, however, has made it increasingly apparent that these institutions have serious constraints as vehicles for on-lending to small enterprises.

Many of these development banks were created and developed through the World Bank's initiatives, encouragement and financial assistance. A recent policy paper by the Bank on the subject of financial intermediation (Financial Intermediation Policy Paper, Industry Department, World Bank, July 1985) has reviewed the role of these institutions over the past decades, and the World Bank's involvement with them, in providing finance for industrial development. Since the early 1960s the World Bank has loaned nearly US$13 billion to over 130 development finance institutions. These loans are estimated to have created over 2.5 million jobs but most of the funds were lent to larger enterprises.

There is no question that development finance institutions have played an important role in financing industrial investment. In many countries they have been an important source of term finance and of foreign exchange as well as generating a pool of trained professionals who can now be found in all financial institutions, industry and government in developing countries. There is also no doubt that many such institutions played a pioneering role by providing finance to small and medium enterprises, even if on a limited basis, when it was not available from other sources.

Despite this important role, recent reviews show that development banks have not been very successful in terms of financial performance. Many of them are today in a serious financial position which in some cases even threatens their very survival. Most such institutions are suffering from heavy arrears on their loans, with more than a quarter of them having more than half their portfolio affected in this way. One sample of such institutions reported that their net income during the period from 1981 to 1983 averaged only 0.8 per cent of their total assets and even this figure may not reflect the true situation because in most cases inadequate provision was made for losses. Development finance institutions definitely fared badly in the economic shocks of the early 1980s.

It is generally accepted that development banks were not created to maximize profitability and that their development orientation should be paramount. Nevertheless, one major objective of the World Bank's lending to such institutions, and indeed that of most other international financial agencies, is that they become 'independent' financial organizations capable of mobilizing resources on their own. Without a minimum level of profitability there is virtually no chance of mobilizing commercial resources and this means that the institutions remain dependent on international aid programmes and government funding. Many of them are indeed in such a position.

Part of their problem was that they made loans on which the income was insufficient to cover operating costs or to provide for the inherent risks, and this applies particularly to some of their small enterprise financing activities. If small enterprise lending is to be profitable, the spreads have to be significantly higher than those obtained on loans to larger firms.

There are other reasons, apart from their difficult financial situation and limited resources, that have led the World Bank to conclude that these institutions are not the most suitable ones for channelling finance to small enterprises. They are usually very centralized and lack the branch network that is needed to respond quickly to the demands of small business. In most countries they are either not allowed, or find it impossible, to mobilize local funding through deposits, and thus cannot meet the working capital needs of small enterprises. Most such clients prefer to deal with a single financial institution that can meet all their financial requirements. Also development banks have evolved appraisal systems that require documentation and data which is far beyond the capacity of small enterprises and which has resulted in slow processing of loan requests which is quite unrelated to the needs of small borrowers.

MULTI-INSTITUTIONAL LENDING FOR SMALL BUSINESS

For the above reasons the World Bank has, since the late 1970s, chosen in most of its small enterprise support projects to rely mainly on commercial banks as the channels for providing loans to small business through multi-institutional refinancing arrangements. Typically, these arrangements allow eligible commercial and development banks to use a fund which has been set up either in the central bank of the country or in another designated apex-institution, which may also be a development bank.

These loans are in turn on-lent to small enterprises by any of the participating institutions, usually commercial banks but sometimes also other financing institutions, such as credit unions, and are then refinanced, either on a 100 per cent (or in some cases 80 per cent) basis, from a special fund in the apex-institution. This refinancing arrangement, which means that the on-lending institutions do not have to use their own resources, has proved effective in many countries in bringing commercial banks into the field of lending to small business. Development banks have also been encouraged to participate in these schemes to add a development orientation and a preparedness to be less stringent in demanding collateral and in financing new businesses. The commercial banks are encouraged to compete with each other in the use of these funds, and the World Bank is thus protected from being too dependent on a single institution.

These arrangements encourage commercial banks to lend to small businesses but do not solve all the major problems of credit to small enterprises. There is still a problem of the spread to be allowed to the participating banks. While some such schemes have operated on spreads of 2 and 3 per cent, this has proved to be inadequate and some commercial banks have as a result stopped their operations in this field. Alternatively, some banks limit their lending to their well-known and credit-worthy clients and reduce the time their staff spend on assisting borrowers with project preparation, or in appraisal and supervision. In such circumstances the commercial banks are only participating because of their interest in developing a wider clientele for the use of other financial services. They remain cautious, by insisting on short repayment periods and adequate collateral.

TRANSACTION COSTS

The transaction costs of lending to small enterprises are bound to be high, because of the small amounts involved in each loan. Additionally, greater administrative effort is required to obtain the necessary documentation and data on which to base decisions, and supervision and collection are also often more expensive than when loans are made to larger enterprises.

In order to be profitable, institutions which lend to small enterprises must obtain an income from the interest which covers the cost of the funds being used, the transaction costs, some provision for losses due to defaults and some marginal profit. To achieve this, lenders to small enterprises must

receive a relatively higher spread. Some studies in the
Philippines in the 1970s found that transaction costs in
lending to small businesses were of the order of 2.5 per cent
to 3 per cent of the value of the loans, as opposed to less
than 0.5 per cent on loans to large businesses ('Transactions
costs of Credit to the small scale sector in the Philippines',
K. Saito and D.P. Villanueva, World Bank, 1978). Other studies
in Colombia and in Asian countries have shown that the
transaction costs are more in the order of 5 per cent to 7 per
cent and this is probably a more realistic figure when dealing
with a widely dispersed clientele which includes a proportion
of new enterprises.

The spreads obtained by institutions lending to small
enterprises clearly have to be sufficient to cover these costs,
and losses, and in most loans being made by the World Bank in
the last few years the spreads have been in the range of 5 per
cent to 8 per cent. Such high levels raise serious financial
questions, since they sometimes can only be achieved by
allowing the banks to on-lend at higher interest rates than
those prevailing in the commercial markets, or by subsidizing
the funds which are made available for on-lending to small
business.

It is important to sound a word of caution on the issue of
transaction costs and increased spread. While higher costs are
inherent in the nature of small business lending, it is
important not to allow this to conceal higher costs which arise
from weak management, poor staffing and inefficient procedures.
In small enterprise lending programmes, as in any other type of
activity, it is always possible to achieve greater efficiency
and reduce costs.

INTEREST RATES

The World Bank believes that funds provided for on-lending to
small enterprises should be lent at a positive real interest
rate, as related to the level of inflation in the country and
to the rates prevailing in commercial credit markets. The Bank
has conducted a dialogue on this policy for some years with
different countries, and has also pressed that the rates should
be appropriately higher than those offered by institutions for
deposits. In general, for political and social reasons it has
been considered unacceptable by governments to lend to small
enterprises at a higher interest rate than to larger borrowers.
In practice, because it is more expensive to lend to small
enterprises, they are already receiving an implicit subsidy
when they borrow at the same rate as larger firms.

It has not proved easy to persuade all developing countries
that access to institutional finance is more important to small
enterprises than the level of interest. Gradually, however, as
experience accumulates, many governments in developing
countries are coming to recognize the disadvantages of
subsidized on-lending rates. In particular, it has become

apparent that subsidized interest rates erode the capital of the fund from which the loans are being made, since repayments are never able to replace the real value. A representative of a Latin American country gave a vivid account of such fund erosion at a recent regional meeting, when he recounted how a fund for small enterprises that had been lent at subsidized rates was, when it had been fully repaid, worth less than 5 per cent of its original value. Studies in other Latin American countries show that many other such funds have lost more than 60 per cent of their original value by the time they have been repaid. The inevitable results of such operations is to prevent the on-lending institution from achieving any degree of self financing, and to condemn it to continuous dependence on government or overseas aid sources.

There are, of course, other effects of on-lending at subsidized interest rates. There is repeated evidence of major distortions in the use of such loans and in the types of beneficiaries who benefit. Such subsidized lending programmes benefit the wealthy and politically influential rather than those who really need the funds and can make best use of them. Even in situations where the funds are actually used for the purposes for which they are requested, which it is claimed can be controlled, it is inevitable that such loans are taken up by those who could use other available finance for investments. They find it financially advantageous to use their own funds for other purposes. The loans thus fail to achieve any genuine 'additionality' and simply replace other resources.

Subsidized loans can also make projects appear viable when, if they were to be judged by the real cost of money, they are in fact unprofitable. These subsidies also lead to investments in equipment which cannot be properly utilized and encourage capital- rather than labour-intensive technology. This works against one of the main ojectives of small enterprise lending which is to create employment. Finally, to compound the problem, there is clear evidence that subsidized interest rates often lead to poor repayment. In periods of financial difficulty, the more expensive loans are quite rationally repaid first.

For all the above reasons the World Bank opposes subsidized interest rates. If governments discard the option of allowing financial institutions to charge higher interest rates to small borrowers, the only remaining possibility is to provide funds at lower costs to the lending institutions so that they can attain the spread which is necessary to cover the higher transaction costs and risks.

FOREIGN EXCHANGE RISKS

Changes in the foreign exchange value of the local currency complicates the on-lending to small enterprises of funds which have been lent by the World Bank and other donor agencies, since such loans must be repaid in foreign currency. The World

Bank has generally adopted the policy that development finance institutions should pass on this foreign exchange risk to their borrowers, so that the loans have to be repaid as though they were denominated in foreign currency. In the case of small enterprise lending, where the loans to small borrowers are always made in local currency, this policy has never, except in the case of Korea, been applied. The foreign exchange risk has been borne by governments. Small enterprises are unable to cope with the problem of changes in foreign exchange rates and have on occasions refused to borrow unless they are aware of their exact debt obligations in advance.

In many countries, however, where there are repeated devaluations and volatile currencies, the assumption of the foreign exchange risk by government implies a major subsidy. For this reason, it is impossible to separate foreign exchange risk and interest rates. If the interest rate charged is positive in real terms the effect of changes in foreign exchange rates will have been taken into account. In the all too frequent situations, however, of sharp changes in currency values and very rapid inflation, it becomes increasingly difficult to make the necessary abrupt changes in interest rates. It is even more difficult to predict inflation trends, which is necessary if interest rates are to be set correctly.

The ideal solution would then be for loans to be made at variable interest rates linked to a price index, but in most cases this is just as unacceptable to small scale borrowers as would be their assumption of the foreign exchange risk. The government of Ecuador have recently agreed to introduce variable interest rates on loans to small enterprises, and it has been proposed, but not yet agreed, that the interest charges should be capitalized in order to ease the repayments by the borrower. Such an expedient is usually impossible, however, and the institution is forced to the second best solution of gradually raising interest rates by stages on new loans in order to reach a positive real level. In addition, a foreign exchange risk fee can be charged but this is generally far from adequate to compensate government for the high cost of bearing the risk when there are major devaluations. In countries with very volatile exchange rates and high rates of inflation, the World Bank generally insists on frequent reviews in order to have interest rates adjusted as the situation changes.

GRACE PERIODS AND MATURITIES

The cash flow needed to service a loan may for small firms be more important than the interest rate which is charged. Cash flow is largely a function of loan maturities and grace periods. Even when high interest rates are charged, a package of appropriate grace and repayment periods can make the repayments within the debt servicing capacity of the enterprise, whereas even low interest rates may cause problems if there is no grace period and the maturity is short.

The grace period and maturities of a given loan are often determined by the particular needs of the lender, such as the repayment conditions which may have been imposed by the source of funds. They may also be influenced by the lender's perception of the capacity and the reliability of the borrower to pay. Eventually, by enforcing shorter maturities the lender may compound a borrower's problems and make him even less able to repay. The general financial situation and the lender's perception of likely future rates of inflation may make the future cost of funds needed to replace those being on-lent uncertain, and thus influence the repayment periods which are set.

As most loans are designated for specific purposes it is logical for loans for working capital to be repaid more quickly than loans for fixed assets. There is a similar rationale for relating the repayment to the life of the assets being financed. There is also a strong case for allowing grace periods on loans made to finance equipment, at least to cover the period until the new machinery starts operations. Many arrears, particularly in the case of new enterprises, arise from inadequate grace periods.

Commercial banks are generally strongly opposed to borrowing short and lending long, so that funds generated by short-term deposits are inevitably used to make loans for working capital, with short repayment periods. For this reason, if commercial or development banks are expected to make long-term loans to small enterprises, they will clearly have to be provided with funds with repayment periods and interest rates which make it possible for them to be on-lent on conditions suitable for small scale borrowers.

RISK SHARING

Even when small scale loans are made through refinancing schemes, the risk still remains with the on-lending institution which naturally seeks to cover itself by requiring collateral. This inevitably limits access to such funds to small scale entrepreneurs who are able to furnish such collateral.

In some countries efforts have been made to solve this problem, and to provide finance for small scale entrepreneurs with good projects but inadequate collateral, through risk sharing arrangements which are usually in the form of credit guarantee schemes. Such schemes guarantee the lender against defaults, generally up to 70 to 80 per cent of the loss incurred. The government, or sometimes the banks, local governments or other associations, create a fund for this purpose. In most cases a fee is charged to the lender, the borrower or both, mainly to cover the costs of the scheme's administration. These schemes are intended to encourage commercial banks to lend to small enterprises but they also are intended to reduce the costs of such lending by substantially reducing the risk of losses.

It is interesting to note that in industrialized countries guarantee schemes are the main form of government assistance for small enterprise financing. In some countries, such as Holland and Canada, there is no actual fund, but the government undertakes to cover the losses.

In developing countries such schemes have had less success. In most cases the commercial banks do not have confidence that the claims will be met and are reluctant to face the bureaucratic delays and arguments associated with making claims. While such schemes can play an important role in broadening the access of small enterprises to institutional finance, it should be recognized that there are problems in their practical implementation, and that their introduction can increase the costs and delays involved in lending to small enterprises.

The whole issue of risks raises the question of what is an acceptable level of arrears or default for this type of lending. Even in industrialized countries it is stated that between 30 per cent and 50 per cent of all new small businesses fail, and it is unrealistic to expect a higher rate of success in developing countries. In small enterprise lending programmes careful selection and appraisal of projects, together with some technical assistance, can help to reduce the number of defaults and failures. Nevertheless, a higher arrears rate must be expected on small enterprise lending, not because small firms are more negligent but because they are more affected by external factors.

The risk of losses increases if more loans are given to new enterprises or first time entrepreneurs. The loss rate can be reduced by lending only to existing enterprises with good past records of repayment, as done by some commercial banks, but this fails to meet the development needs in many developing countries where there is a major social and economic need to widen the basis of entrepreneurial activity. If higher arrears and default rates are accepted in small enterprise lending, this must have important implications for the incomes of the lending institutions.

THE SUSTAINABILITY OF SMALL ENTERPRISE LENDING SCHEMES

As has already been stated, one of the aims of lending schemes for small enterprises is that they should eventually be self-financing and sustainable without continuous recourse to external sources of funds. Since it is perceived as expensive and unprofitable to lend to small enterprises, there is little incentive for either commercial or development banks to use their own resources for this purpose. Some small enterprise lending programmes force the lenders to use some of their own resources by refinancing only 80 per cent or less of their loans. This is reinforced by a general agreement that the total amount lent will only finance 70 per cent or 80 per cent of the project cost, the rest of the money having to be invested by the entrepreneur himself in the form of equity from his own funds. This is already a high debt equity ratio for those starting in business for the first time.

It is to be hoped that as institutions acquire greater experience in lending to small enterprises and are thus able to reduce administrative costs and risks, by selecting credit worthy borrowers and viable projects, they will also be prepared to use more of their own funds. It has also been suggested that central banks and governments might encourage commercial banks in particular to use more of their own resources for small enterprise lending by offering to pay back to these banks a sum which is equivalent to an agreed interest rebate on all loans made to small enterprises from the banks' own funds.

Some countries claim to have solved, or at least partially solved, this problem by saying that a certain proportion of all commercial bank lending must go to small businesses. Such regulations it is claimed have been a success in India, but in other cases it has been found difficult to enforce them. In developing countries, bank operations are usually weakly supervised, and mandatory quotas of lending have in some cases led to undesirable distortions in credit allocation.

Commercial banks, as opposed to development banks, are more able to cover the costs of lending to small enterprises from other income, because of the variety of services they offer, but they are reluctant to cross-subsidize small enterprise lending. There have, nevertheless, been some cases where commercial banks have operated limited lending programmes to small enterprises, knowing that they will make little or no profit and that they are being subsidized from other income. The purpose may be to reach new clients, or even to show goodwill and to cooperate with government programmes. In the long run, however, such banks will expect to see some direct financial advantages from such lending.

It is less possible for development banks to cover the cost of small enterprise lending from other income. It is possible for development banks to cover their losses through the returns on investment of on-lent funds in safe securities, especially in situations where they are highly liquid. Some other institutions attempt to raise income through charging commissions or fees for appraisal and supervision and penalty interest charges on arrears, which are also, of course, levied as a deterrent. Such penalty interest charges are often not realized, and are in fact no more than illusory income. In general, development banks have little opportunity for raising revenues from other sources and are therefore more dependent than commercial banks on an adequate spread to cover the costs of lending to small enterprises.

CONCLUSIONS

The appropriate arrangements for small enterprise lending will vary from country to country depending on the operations of financial markets and the prevailing financial and economic conditions and the institutional framework. In some countries, in Africa, for instance, the financial sector and commercial banking system are so underdeveloped that despite all the limitations a development bank is the only possible vehicle for channelling funds to small enterprises. In some other situations, the only possibility may be to attempt to channel credit through a small enterprise promotion institution, created to foster small enterprise development in general. It is only possible to evaluate lending programmes on a long-term basis, but whenever feasible the multi-institutional approach of channelling funds through both commercial and development banks through refinancing schemes seems to be the most effective arrangement. Loans to small enterprises must be made on conditions which are within the debt servicing capacity of the borrowers and in a form to make it possible for the lending institutions to develop programmes which are ultimately self sustaining.

INTRODUCTION

As mentioned earlier, there were three occasions for discussion, one after each of the sub-themes, which were themselves introduced by two or three papers. The discussions altogether lasted around four hours.

All the papers covered a wider range of subjects than the respective sub-theme, and the attempt to divide this seminar into the three components of income, revenue and expenses was somewhat artificial since they are closely interrelated and each requires a number of assumptions to be made about the type of organization, the target group and so on. This summary attempts to do justice both to the actual discussions and to the sub-themes on which they were based.

The first part of the summary covers the discussions concerning institutional constraints and possibilities. As already stated in the introduction, the definition of SSE-DFI given by the FMO proved to be too limiting. In the second part, we have brought together the two different types of pricing, namely the interest rate charged by the lending institution to the client, including some attention to the risk element, and the price charged by the suppliers of funds to the lending institution. In this latter aspect, we are also concerned with the necessity or otherwise of subsidies.

The third part of the summary covers those aspects which are related to the actual operations of an SSE-DFI such as screening, appraisal and follow-up, without going into very much detail on the specific costs related to each of these activities.

No clear-cut solutions or single best answers to the problems of SSE-financing evolved from the discussions. Nevertheless, some lines of common thinking appeared to develop and the Chairman summarized these in his concluding remarks, which are given in the fourth part of this summary.

INSTITUTIONS

The institution providing finance to small-scale enterprises determines to a large extent both the types and number of small-scale enterprises which gain effective access to credit. The best organization to work with a small-scale enterprise may indeed be another small-scale enterprise or, if it must be a large organization, still a business. Highly centralized government agencies often do more harm than good to the development of small-scale enterprises. If this is accepted, it could follow that small-scale banks should be promoted; if they are profitable, larger commercial banks within due course will follow their example in lending to small enterprises.

Nevertheless, it was felt that the concept of a small-scale

enterprise is not the same as a small-scale bank. SSE-DFIs are top-down institutions, which closely resemble their parent development finance companies. In the long run, an SSE-DFI has to be substantially modified if it is to become functional.

Small-scale banks are far more similar to the local entrepreneurial banks which eventually came together to establish the Bank for Small and Medium Business (NMB) in The Netherlands. In developing countries the traditional moneylenders perform many of the functions of a small bank. Their scope and mode of operations, however, makes them part of the informal sector.

Participants referred repeatedly to the potential of the commercial banks as sources of finance for small enterprise. Nevertheless, experience in countries such as Liberia and elsewhere shows that such banks are either unable or unwilling to finance small enterprises. On occasion they even appear to be exploitative rather than development oriented, and there is no alternative but to create a new institution to finance small enterprises.

In some other countries commercial banks do provide credit to small enterprises, mainly on a short-term basis, while DFIs provide the investment capital. Commercial banks are therefore not able to provide all the finance which small enterprises need.

In the World Bank experience a system whereby credit is made available to small enterprises from an apex organization, through commercial banks, can evolve in one of two different ways. If only a few banks participate and they each use quite a sizeable part of the credit facility, they modify their organization accordingly: special staff are trained, a department is created and technical assistance may even be provided. When many banks participate, however, each lending small amounts to small enterprises, organizational changes do not appear to be justified.

In Liberia, the World Bank works with an SSE-DFI. If Liberian commercial banks change their present attitude, the World Bank will be pleased to see them making use of its facilities. No organization can claim exclusive rights based on historical working agreements. The World Bank is interested in the widest possible institutional participation.

Most participants would agree that commercial banks have in principle all the advantages when it comes to financing small enterprises; they know their environment and they know the people, as was borne out by the history of the entrepreneurial banks in The Netherlands. They have a widespread branch network, which gives them the proximity to small enterprises which is perhaps the most crucial factor in working successfully with them. Finally, they have local currency resources.

Nevertheless, commercial banks are not eager to lend to small enterprises, because of their perception of the risks and of the costs involved. As a result, it seems obvious to attempt to diminish the risk by providing guarantees, and to subsidize some of the costs which are necessarily higher per unit of account lent to small businesses than for large ones.

The centralized approach, which is virtually innate to development finance companies and up to now also characterizes SSE-DFIs, will probably not function effectively in the long run. It has to be accepted that even after 25 years many development finance companies still have major problems. It may be that these companies should attempt to change the attitude of the commercial banks, or should combine their strength, namely their intimate knowledge of investment banking, with the strengths of the commercial banks.

Nevertheless, it seems premature at this time to rely only on commercial banks. The experience in Sri Lanka bears this out. The small and medium industry department of the Development Finance Corporation of Ceylon is now a very effective and large-scale user of the World Bank's line of credit for small enterprises, and is even more active than one of the two large commercial banks with more than 300 branches. This bears out the point which was made earlier, namely that competition is as desirable in lending to small enterprises as in any other economic activity.

PRICING

Since the viability of small enterprise financing institutions depends on the price they pay for their resources and the price they charge for their loans, these two issues were discussed at some length.

FMO stated that in the long run it wll not provide subsidized funds to SSE-DFIs for on-lending. It is important to make a clear distinction between the financial function and the non-financial services; the latter will clearly continue to need subsidy. Before the lending function, however, reaches its breakeven point, concessional funds or subsidies are needed. During the initial phases of developing a new institution income will never cover expenses. This is even truer when one is trying to build a new professional banking institution.

Although most participants agreed with this view in principle, it appeared in discussion that many participants believed that the financing function would need to be subsidized in the long term. All were agreed, however, that any subsidy should be explicit and visible, for specific purposes and a specific period of time. If this is not done, subsidies generate a life of their own and management are tempted to see them as an easy escape from their problems.

It is unrealistic to expect bankers to finance small enterprises unless some form of subsidy is available. They must be lent funds at lower than prevailing rates, or they should be able to on-lend the funds at higher than normal interest rates. There is no doubt that the transaction costs involved in lending to small businesses are higher, and that this type of lending is perceived, rightly or wrongly, to be more risky. A credit guarantee scheme can cope with many problems. Technical assistance in itself does not make small enterprise financing attractive or viable for a bank. It may be necessary but is not a sufficient condition for a viable SSE-DFI. In addition, concessional funding for SSE-DFIs can be justified because it is a means of providing credit to enterprises which would otherwise not obtain it, and more enterprises do become involved in the economy which benefits the economic development in general. Subsidies may eventually, of course, be recovered from the taxes that are paid by the new businesses.

It could also be argued that the very concept of development involves subsidies, since otherwise the activity in question would already be taking place. If we feel that there should be more credit available to small enterprises, some element of subsidy must be provided. The question is not whether such lending should be subsidized, but how.

If every aspect of small enterprise promotion is to be viable, it was argued, the total price would be too high. In Africa, in particular, this is not a feasible approach. Development necessarily involves subsidy, but this must not jeopardize the continuity of what is being attempted. New and existing enterprises must be financed, and entrepreneurs in developing countries cannot be expected to do better than their colleagues in industrialized nations where up to half of all new businesses fail during the first few years of their existence. If small enterprise promotion is not subsidized in some way, it cannot be done at all.

The exchange risk involved in borrowing foreign resources is a special issue. Donors may offer attractive interest rates, but if the funds must be repaid in the original currency the risk may be such that these loans are nevertheless unattractive. More investigation is needed into swaps and other ways of avoiding this problem.

Some people feel that foreign exchange values are a government responsibility, and that they should therefore bear the risk. Failing that, it is argued, the ultimate borrower should do it; under no circumstances should the lending institution bear the risk of foreign exchange losses.

According to an opposite view, governments are bureaucratic and ponderous, and may also acquire undue influence in the affairs of the lending institution if they bear the foreign exchange risk. For this reason, a number of the lending institutions represented at the seminar do in fact carry this risk, in spite of the World Bank's advice. In general, they justify this by their need to press ahead with the task of lending money, without external interference.

INTEREST RATES

Although there is widespread agreement that real positive interest rates should be charged to entrepreneurs, it is not easy to decide what actual rate should be charged in a specific country at a particular time. Traditional moneylenders charge between 80 per cent in Liberia and over 1000 per cent in Peru. Official institutions, on the other hand, are in most countries limited in their freedom to set interest rates at a real positive level.

This issue is a very difficult one. In countries with hyper-inflation and sharp devaluations, for instance, it is difficult to achieve a real positive interest rate and impossible to agree on what the interest rate should be. Variable interest rates might appear to be the logical answer, but this is difficult for entrepreneurs and governments alike to accept. The World Bank has, however, achieved a breakthrough with this approach in Ecuador, where the concept was accepted after lengthy discussions.

Transitional strategies may be necessary in order to achieve gradual change, in the hope that a government will take appropriate measures to stabilize the currency. Sudden changes are out of the question, but it may be possible to charge positive real interest rates after a period of two or three years. In other countries, however, real interest rates are too high, and they should be reduced.

It may, therefore, not always be correct to follow the rate of interest charged by the commercial banks. In Ghana, for instance, the agriculture bank charges nine per cent on its loans to farmers; the commercial banks charge 28 per cent to small businesses. Would 14 per cent or 16 per cent be more correct? It is necessary to be flexible, and in some countries, depending on circumstances, it may be necessary to subsidize interest rates to a certain degree.

The difference between formal commercial rates and subsidized rates is far less than that between either of them and the informal market. If moneylenders are charging 80 per cent, is 79 per cent acceptable? The whole issue can be approached not from the angle of what is acceptable, but what rate is necessary to enable the SSE-DFI to be viable. Interest rates must then be set to cover the cost of unsubsidized funds, plus the full transaction costs and bad debts. In Liberia, for instance, this would lead to a rate of around 40 per cent which is considerably lower than moneylenders charge, but more than twice the rate charged by commercial banks.

It can also be argued that interest rates should vary according to the degree of risk; in this case, different borrowers would pay different rates of interest. This approach was not discussed at any length, but it led inevitably to the subject of security, since many entrepreneurs cannot offer sufficient collateral. If SSE-DFIs and commercial banks really are to emphasize development, a guarantee scheme may be part of what is needed. In Thailand the development bank, together with the commercial banks, has set up a credit guarantee scheme which compensates for the lack of collateral and encourages commercial banks to make use of their extensive branch network and access to domestic resources by going into small enterprise lending whole-heartedly.

In the World Bank's experience, guarantee schemes have proved useful but not profitable. If they are profitable, they fail to achieve a development role and do not compensate for the lack of collateral. The cost of running a credit guarantee scheme should be borne totally by local sources such as government and banks, and not by donors. The World Bank, and USAID, are willing to assist in setting up such schemes.

Group guarantees are another way of providing security. This approach is used by the Grameen Bank in Bangladesh, and by BAAC in Thailand. The Central de Credito de Cooperativo in Peru has also had favourable experience in working with solidarity groups of this kind, but it has not been substantiated that this approach is suitable for modern small enterprises as opposed to informal sector micro-enterprises.

In Zambia the SSE-DFI shares the risk by participating in the equity of client enterprises. No dividends are expected for the first five years, but an agreement is made that the shares can be repurchased by the entrepreneur at a price which will give a sufficient profit to the SSE-DFI. This scheme is only in its infancy, however, and experience with venture capital in Mexico and elsewhere has been disappointing. It is also possible to provide finance to small enterprises through leasing, and this is extensively done in Thailand. It is not clear how the security issue affects the interest rates, and this topic was not discussed in any detail.

The Barclays Bank Development Fund, which is a socially motivated programme, adopts what is almost a reverse approach to setting interest rates when compared with that of the commercial banks. Interest rates vary not according to the risk but to the financial structure and burden of financial charges to be borne by the enterprise. If a business has a low equity base and the entrepreneurs main input is labour, a high rate of interest would make the business unviable, because of its high gearing, and a lower rate is therefore charged. If on the other hand there is a low ratio of debt to equity, a higher rate of interest is charged. The development value of the business is thus given prime importance. Barclays Bank itself, of course, does not operate on this principle.

In general, participants seemed to conclude that interest rates should be as close as possible to market rates, in order not to distort relative prices, but that some degree of subsidy in financing might be justified in view of policy changes and exchange rate fluctuations which so often cause damage to small enterprises.

Non-financial services need not be a burden, and can actually contribute to the income of an SSE-DFI. In Zambia, for instance, the SSE-DFI uses its preferential access to foreign currency to operate a wholesale supply business for its clients, and management and accounting services are provided virtually at cost. This component may also in time become self-supporting. In Botswana, seminars appear to be a useful source of finance for the SSE-DFI, and subsidies are therefore not automatic. There are other ways of covering the losses which may be involved in the actual financing operations.

When discussing subsidies participants agreed that it is most important to distinguish clearly between the actual lending operation and the software of technical and related services. When both types of service are provided by the same organization, it is vital that they should be separately costed and that different sources of funds should be used. Both may need subsidies, but these should be controlled at the level of the institution and not of the borrower. In this way, it would be possible to limit and eventually eliminate such subsidies as they cease to be required.

OPERATIONAL ASPECTS

Screening and appraisal

The first criterion in the lending decision must be the personality of the entrepreneur. If he or she is already known to be a responsible manager, the screening procedure can be short. When the SSE-DFI itself is a new institution, as it usually is, the process must take longer since there is no basis of experience.

In Liberia, for example, it is essential to screen and appraise loans carefully, but it is also very time-consuming. Statistical information may not be available, but analysts have to write up the project in some detail, in a way which is completely academic to the entrepreneur. Now that the Business Advisory Service (BAS) has been established as a subsidiary to the SSE-DFI in Liberia, the situation is rather different; BAS works with the entrepreneur before the loan application is made, to develop a workable plan out of the original ideas.

In Zambia, a similar approach is followed and the SSE-DFI works together with the entrepreneur to keep records of his or her business as a preparation for applying for a loan. This not only trains the entrepreneur, but also allows the institution to acquire a good insight into the entrepreneur and the project in order to make a decision. On the same basis, some institutions ask applicants to produce certain data before a particular deadline. If appointments are kept and the requirements are satisfactorily completed, this gives some indication as to the reliability of the applicant.

In Liberia, seven out of ten applications are rejected before formal appraisal starts. In Malawi, less than one out of ten applications reach the Board. In the Philippines, the Planters Development Bank keeps no records of original applications, since most requests are rejected after the first contact between the applicant and the branch manager.

As is indicated by the procedure followed in Liberia, Zambia and Malawi, some months may elapse between the time of original application and the final decision. The first ideas put forward by applicants may not stand investigation, and some ideas can never be developed into a business plan. In other cases, the applicants are found not to be credit worthy even if they have good ideas.

The procedures and times taken differ between institutions and even between individual applications depending on the applicants and their proposals. The time taken obviously depends also on the number of applications in the pipeline. In the Philippines at present, where the economic conditions are bad, it takes less than a month to approve a loan after the completed documentation has been received by the bank. When economic conditions were more favourable, the process took far longer.

Participants had different opinions on the issue of the necessity for speed. Some warned against excessive haste; it takes time to separate the good from the bad applicants, and to distinguish entrepreneurs from opportunists. If a long-term banking relationship is envisaged, it is important to develop this over a period of time before sealing it with a loan. If the process takes too long, however, the more effective entrepreneurs will find alternative sources of finance. It could also be argued that entrepreneurs will be willing to wait if the rate of interest is sufficiently low.

If alternative sources of finance are available at a price similar to that charged by the SSE-DFI, the entrepreneur will opt for the fastest decision maker; he or she may even be willing to pay a premium for speed, as many do to a leasing company in Thailand which charges two or three per cent higher than the prevailing interest rates, but which makes decisions within days because no securities or titles are needed.

A great deal depends on the number of small enterprises applying for a credit. In Sri Lanka so many applications are received that the SSE-DFI can afford only to take the best, and can then also process them within a month. Rejection rates are high, but because of the large numbers of applicants the SSE-DFI can afford this.

In Peru, the cooperative bank screens projects in two ways: first of all they are checked with SENATI, the government sponsored technical assistance training institute and with other agencies with which the entrepreneur may have developed a relationship; and secondly applicants are asked to participate in one of the training courses which the bank organizes for its members. The latter approach appears to be very useful, and is not costly.

None of the institutions represented use psychological tests as a way of screening applicants. The International Labour Office studied eight different business creation programmes and concluded that psychological procedures do no harm but appear not to be very useful either. The results of the control groups did not deviate significantly from those which were selected using psychological tests.

None of the SSE-DFIs represented at the seminar make calculations of the economic rate of return of projects which are put to them. The World Bank sometimes provides development finance corporations with information on sectors to which it has applied shadow pricing techniques, but it would be far too cumbersome to do the same for individual small enterprises. Many SSE-DFIs require applicants to provide information about the employment and the balance of payment effects on their businesses, mainly at the instigation of donor agencies. The screening and appraising of projects, important as they are, can only be judged when the loans have to be collected.

Supervision, Follow-up and Arrears

Appraisal and supervision are too often regarded as different activities which have to be executed by separate departments within the SSE-DFI, or any other banking institutions. It was suggested that in these cases the supervision staff tend to have a lower status than the appraisal staff. This may in part be attributed to the emphasis which is placed by donors in their training programmes on appraisal techniques, perhaps because they are relatively easy to teach. More attention should definitely be given to the management of loans, and skills should be enhanced in this area.

One of the new SSE-DFIs operating in this field has adopted regular procedures in order to work towards creating a sound portfolio. The total portfolio is regularly analysed to see whether the businesses are undercapitalized or suffering in other ways, and whether they need to be revitalized and how. A special collection officer has been appointed which has improved the collection performance, but it is still far from ideal. Re-scheduling proves generally to be a temporary solution since the habit of delayed or non-payment reasserts itself after a short period. A special Business Advisory Service has been created to assist clients, not only at the stage of application but also during the implementation and development of businesses, in addition to the credit provided by the institution. In spite of these improvements, there is no final answer to the development of a sound portfolio. Every institution has to learn for itself, and this is a slow process.

Participants agreed that it is vital to have effective field representation and to be close to the entrepreneurs. A branch network is a major asset for any institution financing small enterprises. There is also a natural relationship between cheap credit and non-repayment; entrepreneurs are sensible people, and will retain cheap credit as long as they can.

Interest penalties may partly solve this problem, but the

general agreement is that cheap credit should be eliminated. One participant remarked that lending money to small enterprises is rather different from selling chewing gum. During the process of screening and appraisal the eventual collection should always be borne in mind. Special police-units or fire brigades do not operate effectively; credit should be based on a relationship of mutual trust between the financier and the entrepreneur.

It was widely agreed that appraisal and supervision should not be separated. One manager from a SSE-DFI who had been thinking of creating a supervision unit in his bank, for instance, decided against this during the discussion. Those who are responsible for supervision and collection have no feeling for the business as such, and it is important to remember that 'any fool can write a loan proposal, but only a good loan officer can collect it'.

CHAIRMAN'S CONCLUDING REMARKS

It is impossible to come up with definite conclusions regarding the issues discussed at the seminar, and in two days all that can be done is to open a few doors, which participants can go through if they think fit. The only way to test the validity of this seminar is to attempt to implement in practice some part at least of what may have been learned. No definite answers were reached, but some general guidelines may have been attained:

- There are no general solutions, and much depends on local circumstances. Above all, the individual enterprise, and the SSE-DFI, depends on the individual who is running it. Theoretically correct procedures are no substitute for effective management.
- The best institution to help a business is another business; SSE-DFIs, and all small business promotion institutions should be run as businesses, in a business-like way.
- SSE-DFIs are not the final answer; they are by no means the only intermediary, and commercial banks should be encouraged to become more involved.
- The arguments against heavily subsidized interest rates are overwhelming; some governments still resist them and must be persuaded otherwise.
- The foreign exchange risk is a real one, when donor funds are involved. SSEs and SSE-DFIs should be insulated from this problem which is not of their own making, and small enterprises generally do not require much foreign exchange in any case.
- Guarantee schemes may be effective, but will need subsidies. These should be 'transparent', since they will otherwise be difficult to stop.
- Non-financial services are generally essential; these can also earn money for the SSE-DFIs themselves.

- The process of appraisal should be as simple as possible with a minimum of paper, analysis and office work. It should be closely tied to the individual, and to the eventual responsibilities of supervision.
- Appraisal and supervision should be carried out by the same person, working in one department.

APPENDIX

SSE-DFI PROFILES

1. SMALL ENTERPRISES FINANCING ORGANIZATION (SEFO) INC.

Monrovia, Liberia
Year of establishment: 1982
Head office: Monrovia
Branches   : Saniquelle
Staff   : 24
Advisors   : 2

Shareholders (30/9/85):   %
    local
    - Liberian Bank for Development and Investment (LBDI)   42
    - Liberian Finance and Trust Corporation (LFTC)   4
    - Agricultural Cooperatives and Development Bank (ACDB) 6
    - National Housing and Savings Bank (NHSB)   6
    - Partnership for Productivity (PfP)/Liberia   2
      foreign
    - Netherlands Development Finance Company (FMO)   40

Donated capital: PfP-International/USAID

Debt financing:

		Foreign Exchange Risk
local:	ACDB	-
	NHSB	-
foreign:	National Bank of Liberia/	-
	The World Bank	
	PfP-International (USAID)	-
	FMO	SEFO

Lending operations: lending limits : US$ 25,000 per project
                  interest rate : 15-21% (dependent on
                  donor)

Portfolio:	approved	disbursed	outstanding
No. of projects	183	178	139
Amount	US$1,849,000	US$1,693,000	US$1,125,960

Collection efficiency: ca. 35% within 3 months (1985)

Complementary Services: Business Advisory Services (BAS)
                     (PfP/USAID)

Special programmes: Market women revolving fund, Monrovia

2. INDEFUND LTD.

Blantyre, Malawi
Year of establishment: 1982
Head Office: Blantyre
Branches : 0
Staff   : 16
Advisors : 1

Shareholders:

	%
local	
- Indebank	62
foreign	
_ FMO	38

Debt financing:

	Foreign Exchange Risk
- FMO	FMO/Indefund
- Kreditanstalt fur Wiederaufbau	Government of Malawi
- USAID	Government of Malawi

Portfolio (31/12/85):	approved	disbursed	outstanding
No. of projects	68	46	46
Amount	MK 2,954,803	MK 1,748,185	MK 1,591,932

Collection efficiency: ca. 75% within 3 months (1985)

Complementary Services: Business Advisory Services (BAS)

(US$1 = MK 1.67 (31.12.1985))

3. SMALL ENTERPRISES FINANCE COMPANY (SEFCO) LTD.

Nairobi, Kenya
Year of establishment: 1979: DFCK, SSI-programme
                       1984: SEFCO Ltd.
Head office: Nairobi
Branches : 0
Staff   : 14
Advisors : 1

Shareholders:

	%
local	
- Development Finance Company of Kenya (DFCK)	54
- Industrial and Commercial Development Corporation (ICDC)	7
foreign	
- Netherlands Development Finance Company (FMO)	31
- Friedrich Ebert Stiftung (FES)	8

Debt financing:

	Foreign Exchange Risk
Treasury/Netherlands	
Government	Netherlands
	Government
FMO	FMO/SEFCO
Barclays Bank	Barclays Bank
Development Fund	Development Fund

Lending operations: lending limits: up to Ksh 1 M.
for expansion: Ksh 1.5 M.
interest rate: 14%

Portfolio	approved	disbursed	outstanding
No. of projects	86	69	69
Amount	Ksh 48.5 M.	Ksh 44.5 M.	Ksh 36 M.

Collection efficiency: ca. 70% (fourth quarter 1985)

Complementary Services: Management Advisory Services
(PfP/USAID)

Special programmes: Working capital guarantee fund in
cooperation with Barclays Bank of Kenya

(US$1 = Ksh 16.21 (31.12.85))

4. TSWELELO PTY LTD.

Gaborone, Botswana
Year of establishment: 1984
Head office: Gaborone
Branches   : Francistown
Staff   : 15
Advisors   : 4

Shareholders

		%
local		
- Botswana Development Corporation (BDC)		35
- National Development Bank		35
foreign		
- Netherlands Development Finance		
Company (FMO)		30

Debt financing:

                                  Foreign Exchange Risk

       local: BDC
     foreign: FMO   Tswelelo/BDC

Lending operations: lending limits: maximum loan size P 100,000
                       interest rate : 18-20%

Portfolio (30/9/85):	approved	disbursed	outstanding
No. of projects	28	22	6
Amount	P766,700	P474,200	P292,500

Collection efficiency: 60%

Complementary Activities: Wholesale company (subsidiary)
                          Factory Sheds
                          Management Advisory Services
                          Seminars

(US$1 = Pula 2.16 (31.12.1985))

5. SMALL-SCALE ENTERPRISES PROMOTION (SEP) LTD.

Lusaka, Zambia
Year of establishment: 1983
Head office : Lusaka
Branches   : 0
Staff   : 6
Advisors   : 2

Shareholders:

	%
local	
– Development Bank of Zambia (DBZ)	25
– Zambia National Commercial Bank (ZNCB)	10
– Zambia Congress of Trade Unions (ZCTU)	15
– Village Industries Services (VIS)	1
foreign	
– Netherlands Development Finance Company (FMO)	24.5
– Friedrich Ebert Stiftung (FES)	24.5

Debt financing:

                                        Foreign Exchange Risk
                    FMO   Government of Zambia

Lending operations: lending limits: Zkwacha 50,000
                    interest rate: 15% (working capital only)

Portfolio	approved	disbursed	outstanding
No. of projects	14	9	9
Share partic.	Zk186,500	Zk117,000	Zk177,000
Amount working			
capital loans	Zk15,200	Zk10,450	Zk10,450

Complementary Services: Wholesale company (subsidiary)
                        Factory sheds (subsidiary)
                        Accountancy services
                        Management Advisory Services

(US$1 = Zkwacha 5.66 (31.12.1985))

6. INDUSTRIAL FINANCE CORPORATION OF THAILAND (IFCT)

Bangkok, Thailand

SSI-Fund
Year of establishment: 1984
Head office: Bangkok
Branches   : 5
Staff   : ca. 25
Advisors   : 0

Financiers

                                        Foreign Exchange Risk

        IFCT   75%
        FMO   25%   IFCT

Lending operations: lending limits: Bt 200,000 - Bt 5,000,000
                    interest rate : 14.5%

Portfolio (30/9/85):	approved	disbursed	outstanding
No. of projects	111	88	88
Amount	Bt 295,740 M.	Bt 191,418 M.	Bt 185,440 M.
Collection efficiency: above 90% within 3 months (1985)			

Complementary activities: Management Advisory Services
                          (via IFCT subsidiary Industrial
                          Management Consultants, IMC)

(US$1 = Baht 26.65 (31.12.1985))

7. DEVELOPMENT FINANCE CORPORATION OF CEYLON (DFCC)
SMALL AND MEDIUM INDUSTRY DEPARTMENT (SMI DEPT.)

Colombo, Sri Lanka

SMI-Dept.
Year of establishment: 1978
Head office: Colombo
Branches   : 0
Staff   : 6
Advisors   : 0

Financiers

local	%	Foreign Exchange Risk
- DFCC	6	
- Central Bank	22	
foreign		
- The World Bank	58	Government of Sri Lanka
- Asian Development Bank	9	Government of Sri Lanka
- FMO	5	Government of Sri Lanka

Lending operations: lending limits: Rs 4M.
                    interest rate : 14%

Portfolio	approved	disbursed	outstanding
No. of projects	304	277	240
Amount	1.560M.	177.7M.	79.8M.

Collection efficiency: 67% (1985)

(US$1 = S.L. Rupee 27.41 (31.12.1985))

8. PLANTERS DEVELOPMENT BANK

Manila, The Philippines
Year of establishment: 1972
Head office: Manila
Branches   : 22 (in 15 provinces)
Staff   : 398
Advisors   : 0

Shareholders

local	%
- Development Bank of the Philippines	26.3
- Private	58.5
foreign	
- FMO	15.2

Debt financing: Deposits and Savings

	Foreign Exchange Risk
- Central Bank of the Philippines (re-discounting)	Government of the Philippines
- Industrial Guarantee Loan Fund (IGLF) - USAID, The World Bank	Government of the Philipines
- Guarantee Fund for Medium & Small Enterprises (GFMSE) - The World Bank	Government of the Philippines
- Agricultural Loan Fund (ALF) - The World Bank	Government of the Philippines
- Development Bank of the Philippines (DBP) (re-discounting)	Government of the Philippines

Lending operations: lending limits: ₱1,000,000 (for SSE only)
interest rate: re-financing: 20-23%
own resources: 24-28%

Portfolio (31/12/85)	approved	disbursed	outstanding
No. of projects	1,015 (1985)	--	2,348
Amount	₱138.4M.	--	₱216M.

Collection efficiency: ca. 73% (last quarter 1985)

Complementary services: Business Advisory Services (branch level)

(US$1 = ₱19.05 31.12.1985))

9. CENTRAL DE CREDITO COOPERATIVO

Lima, Peru
Year of establishment: 1984
Head office: Lima
Branches   : 17
Representative offices: 37
Staff   : 318
Advisors   : 0

Financiers

	%	Foreign Exchange Risk
CCC	67	
FMO	33	FMO/CCC

Lending operations: lending limits: equivalent of US$ 50,000
interest rate : 72-80% effective rate

Portfolio:	approved	disbursed	outstanding
No. of projects	36	34	34
Amount	S/.890 M.	S/.846 M.	S/.846 M.

Collection efficiency: 78%

Complementary activities: Technical Assistance

(US$1 = Sol 17,390 (free market rate as at 31.12.1985))

10. CORPORACION FINANCIERA NACIONAL (CFN) FOPINAR

Quito, Ecuador

FOPINAR - programme for micro-enterprises (apex-institution)
Year of establishment: 1981
Head office: Quito
Network   : all commercial banks in Ecuador
Staff   : 15
Advisors   : 0

Financiers:

	%	Foreign Exchange Risk
CFN	12.5	
IBRD	37.5	Government of Ecuador
FMO	50.0	Government of Ecuador

Lending operations: lending limits: S/.2.5 M.
interest rate : 16%

Portfolio:	approved	disbursed	outstanding
No. of projects	1609	1609	1609
Amount	S/.318 M.	S/.318 M.	S/.318 M.

Complementary services: Technical Assistance
Training Courses for Entrepreneurs

(US$1 = Sucre 124.75 (free market rate as at 31.12.1985))

Wednesday 25 September 1985

10.30	Opening	Mr. Y.B. de Wit
		General Manager FMO
10.45	Introductory remarks	Chairman
11.00	Keynote address	Mr. M.F. de Jong
		Head SSE Department FMO
12.00	Lunch	

14.00   Theme 1: Sources of Income for SSE-DFI

Speakers: Mr. O. Kapijimpanga
General Manager
Small-Scale Enterprises Promotion Ltd.
Lusaka, Zambia

Mr. J. Levitsky
Operations Advisor
Industry Department
The World Bank
Washington D.C., USA

Mr. W. Abel
Kreditanstalt für Wiederaufbau
Frankfurt, Germany

General Discussion

17.00   Adjournment

Thursday 26 September 1985

09.00   Theme 2: Which services do SSE-DFI have to offer SSE?

Speakers: Mr. J.P. Tambunting
President
Planters Development Bank
Manila, The Philippines

Mr. R.M. Morris
Managing Director
Small Enterprises Financing Organization (SEFO) Inc.
Monrovia, Liberia

Mr. Mario Valdez
Head SSE Department
Central de Credito Cooperativo del Peru
Lima, Peru

94

General Discussion

12.00   Lunch

14.00   Theme 3: Sources of Funds available to SSE-DFI

Speakers: Mr. A. Kongsiri
           Executive Vice President
           The Industrial Finance Corporation of Thailand
           Bangkok, Thailand

           Mr. L.P. Reade
           Senior Deputy Asst. Administrator
           Bureau for Private Enterprise
           US Agency for International Development
           Washington D.C., USA

           General Discussion

16.00   Summary and conclusions by the Chairman
16.30   End of Seminar

LIST OF PARTICIPANTS

Mr. W. Abel
Kreditanstalt für Wiederaufbau
Palmengartenstrasse 5-9
D-6000 Frankfurt am Main 1
FEDERAL REPUBLIC OF GERMANY

Dr. B. Adu-Amankwa
Head of Small Scale Enterprises Department
National Investment Bank
P.O. Box 3726
Accra
GHANA

Mr. A.I. Al-Arhabi
General Manager
Industrial Bank of Yemen
P.O. Box 323
Sanaa
YEMEN ARABIC REPUBLIC

Mr. Stein Albregts
Head Small Enterprise Development Section
International Labour Organisation
4, Route des Morillons
CH-1211 Genève 22
SWITZERLAND

Mr. N.G.C. Burrows, General Manager
Tswelelo (Pty) Ltd.
P.O. Box 438
Gaborone
BOTSWANA

Mr. J. Cedergren
Swedish International Development Association
Head of Industry and Infrastructure Division
Birger Jarlsgatan 61
S-10525 Stockholm
SWEDEN

Mr. M.A. Diop
Chef du Départment du Crédit Industriel
   et Touristique
SOFISEDIT
B.P. 2003
Dakar
SENEGAL

Mr. J. P. Dupressoir
Caisse Centrale de Coopération Economique
Cité du Retiro
35-37 Rue Boissy d'Anglas
75379 Paris Cedex 08
FRANCE

Mr. S. Anders Grettve
Swedfund
P.O. Box 16360
S-10327 Stockholm
SWEDEN

Mr. L. Hans
Rabobank Nederland
P.O. Box 17100
3500 HG Utrecht
HOLLAND

Professor M. Harper
Cranfield School of Management
Cranfield, Bedford MK43 OAL
UNITED KINGDOM

Mr. M. Hasdorf
The Industrialization Fund for
  Developing Countries
P.O. Box 2155
DK-1016 Copenhagen K
DENMARK

Mr. G. Heuss and Ms. M. Nimz
German Finance Company for Investments
  in Developing Countries
P.O. Box 450340
D-5000 Köln 51
FEDERAL REPUBLIC OF GERMANY

Mr. M.A. Huybregts
Principal Administrator
Commission of the European Communities
200, Rue de la Loi
1049 Brussels
BELGIUM

Mr. L. Kambuaya
Manager Loan Division
The Irian Jaya Joint Development Foundation
P.O. Box 410
Jayapura, Irian Jaya
INDONESIA

Mr. D.R. Kantembe, Manager
Indefund Ltd.
P.O. Box 2339
Blantyre
MALAWI

Mr. O.L.D. Kapijimpanga
General Manager
Small Scale Enterprises Promotion Ltd.
P.O. Box 36102
Lusaka
ZAMBIA

Mr. A. Kitonyi, Manager
Small Enterprises Finance Company Ltd.
P.O. Box 34045
Nairobi
KENYA

Mr. A. Kongsiri
Executive Vice-President
The Industrial Finance Corporation
  of Thailand
1770 New Petchburi Road
Bangkok 10310
THAILAND

Mr. J. Levitsky
Operations Advisor Industry Department
International Bank for Reconstruction
  and Development
1818 H Street N.W.
Washington, DC 20433
USA

Miss L. Lewis
Assistant Manager
Barclays Bank PLC
54 Lombard Street,
London EC3P 3AH
UNITED KINGDOM

Mr. F.D. van Loon
Netherlands Bank for Small and
  Medium Business (NMB)
P.O. Box 1800
1000 BV Amsterdam
HOLLAND

Mr. J.C. Lorin
Head Industrial Services
Canadian International Development Agency
Place du Centre
200 Promenade du Portage
Hull K1A OG4
Quebec
CANADA

Mr. D.E. de Mel, Manager
Small & Medium Industry Department
Development Finance Corporation of Ceylon
P.O. Box 1397
Colombo 7
SRI LANKA

Ministry of Foreign Affairs
Directorate General for
  Development Cooperation
att. Mr. B.J. Ronhaar
P.O. Box 20061
2500 EB Den Haag
HOLLAND

Mr. R.M. Morris
Managing Director
Small Enterprises Financing Organization
  (SEFO) Inc.
c/o P.O. Box 2647
Monrovia
LIBERIA

Messrs. D. Pratt and D. Stephen
Commonwealth Development Corporation
33, Hill Street
London W1A 3AR
UNITED KINGDOM

Mr. L.P. Reade
Deputy Assistant Administrator
Bureau for Private Enterprise
Agency for International Development
320, 21st Street, N.W.
Washington, D.C. 20523
U.S.A.

Mr. V. Rhone
Trafalgar Development Bank Ltd.
P.O. Box 8927 C.S.O.
Kingston
JAMAICA

Mr. A. Stoll
Friedrich-Ebert-Stiftung
Godesberger Allee 149
5300 Bonn 2
FEDERAL REPUBLIC OF GERMANY

Mr. J.P. Tambunting
Chairman and President
Planters Development Bank
149 Legaspi Street
Legaspi Village
Makati, Metro Manila
THE PHILIPPINES

Mr. Mario Valdez
Director Program CCC-FMO
Central de Credito Cooperativo del Peru
Camilo Carillo 114
Jesús Maria/Lima II
PERU

Mr. F.C.M. Wils
Senior Lecturer Sociology
Institute of Social Studies
P.O. Box 90733
2509 LS Den Haag
HOLLAND

www.ingramcontent.com/pod-product-compliance
Lightning Source LLC
Chambersburg PA
CBHW051612030426
42334CB00035B/3493